A Penguin Special
Mission to South Africa

THE COMMONWEALTH GROUP OF
EMINENT PERSONS

Mission to South Africa

THE COMMONWEALTH REPORT

Foreword by Shridath Ramphal
Commonwealth Secretary-General

Published by Penguin Books
for the Commonwealth Secretariat

Penguin Books Ltd, Harmondsworth, Middlesex, England
Viking Penguin Inc., 40 West 23rd Street, New York, New York, 10010, U.S.A.
Penguin Books Australia Ltd, Ringwood, Victoria, Australia
Penguin Books Canada Limited, 2801 John Street, Markham, Ontario, Canada L3R 1B4
Penguin Books (N.Z.) Ltd, 182–190 Wairau Road, Auckland 10, New Zealand

First published 1986

Made and printed in Great Britain by
Richard Clay (The Chaucer Press) Ltd, Bungay, Suffolk
Typeset in Monophoto Plantin

Contents

ANNEXES

Members of the Commonwealth Group of Eminent Persons: Biographical Details

MR MALCOLM FRASER (CO-CHAIRMAN), Proposed by the Prime Minister of Australia, was the Prime Minister of Australia 1975–83, having held a number of Cabinet positions since 1968. He entered Parliament in 1955, after graduating from Oxford University in 1952. As Prime Minister, Mr Fraser chaired the Commonwealth summit held in Melbourne in 1981 and was responsible for initiating the series of Commonwealth Heads of Government Regional Meetings for the Asia/Pacific region. Lately an International Fellow of Harvard University, Mr Fraser was Chairman of the United Nations Panel of Eminent Persons which recently reported on the Activities of Transnational Corporations in South Africa and Namibia. He is a member of the Inter Action Council of former Heads of Government formed in 1983.

GENERAL OLUSEGUN OBASANJO (CO-CHAIRMAN), proposed jointly by the President of Zambia and the Prime Minister of Zimbabwe, was the head of the Federal Military Government of Nigeria 1976–79, when he handed over power to an elected civilian government, headed by President Shehu Shagari. A Fellow of the University of Ibadan from 1979, General Obasanjo served on the Independent (Palme) Commission on Disarmament and Security, and he is a member of the Inter Action Council of former Heads of Government. As an officer in the Nigerian army, which he joined in 1958, he served with the United Nations forces in the Congo in 1960. He served as Federal Commissioner for Works and Housing in 1975 and was promoted Lt-General in 1976 and General in 1979.

LORD BARBER OF WENTBRIDGE, proposed by the Prime Minister of Britain, has been Chairman of the Standard Chartered Bank since 1974. Having served as Economic Secretary to the British Treasury 1959–62, Financial Secretary to the Treasury 1962–3 and Minister of Health 1963–4, Lord Barber was Chancellor of the Exchequer 1970–74. He was Chairman of the Conservative Party 1967–70 and a member of the Falkland Islands Inquiry Committee (Franks Committee) in 1982. A graduate of Oxford University and a barrister, he entered Parliament in 1951.

DAME NITA BARROW was proposed by the Prime Minister of The Bahamas. A Barbadian national, Dame Nita Barrow was President of the World YWCA 1975–83 and has been a President of the World Council of Churches since 1983 and President of the International Council for Adult Education since 1982. She was the convener of the Non-Governmental Organizations Forum

for the World Conference to review the United Nations Decade for Women held in Nairobi in 1985. After being Principal Nursing Officer in Jamaica and Nursing Adviser to the Pan-American Health Organization for the Commonwealth Caribbean, she served as Associate Director (1972–5) and as Director (1975–81) of the Christian Medical Commission of the World Council of Churches in Geneva. She was made a Dame of St Andrew in 1980.

MR JOHN MALECELA, proposed by the President of Zambia and the Prime Minister of Zimbabwe, was Foreign Minister of Tanzania 1972–5. He later held other positions in the Cabinet (Agriculture 1978–80, Minerals 1980–82, Communications and Transport 1982–4 and Communications and Works 1984–5) until he relinquished office at the end of 1985. He was Vice-Chairman of the Independent (Maitland) Commission for Worldwide Telecommunications Development. As Tanzania's Permanent Representative at the United Nations 1964–8, Mr Malecela was elected Chairman of the United Nations Committee on Decolonization in 1967. He was a Minister in the East African Community before becoming a Minister in Tanzania in 1972. He studied at the Universities of Bombay and Cambridge.

SARDAR SWARAN SINGH, proposed by the Prime Minister of India, has been in public life since 1946 and served as India's Minister of External Affairs 1964–6 and 1970–74 and as Minister of Defence 1966–70 and 1974–5. He had held a number of other portfolios in the Indian Government from 1952 onwards. A leader of the Indian delegation to the United Nations General Assembly on eight occasions, he was elected to the Executive Board of UNESCO in 1985. He was a member of the United Nations Panel of Eminent Persons on Regional and Inter-regional Co-operation 1982–4 and has been Co-Chairman of the Policy Board of the Inter Action Council since 1983. He played an active role during the Indian Freedom movement and was in charge of legal defence of all political activists of all parties. He was on the Partition Committee of the Punjab.

THE MOST REVEREND EDWARD WALTER SCOTT, proposed by the Prime Minister of Canada, has been the Primate of the Anglican Church of Canada since 1971. Educated at the University of British Columbia and the Anglican Theological College of British Columbia, he was ordained in 1942. He served as Director of Social Service and Priest-in-Charge of Indian Work in the Diocese of Rupertsland 1960–64 and Associate Secretary of the Council for Social Service of the Anglican Church 1964–6 and was Bishop of Kootenay

On the steps of Marlborough House. Left to right: Mr Shridath Ramphal, Commonwealth Secretary-General; Archbishop Ted Scott, Canada; Dame Nita Barrow, Co-President, World Council of Churches, Barbados; Mr Malcolm Fraser, former Prime Minister, Australia; General Olusegun Obasanjo, former Head of State, Nigeria; Lord Barber, former Chancellor of the Exchequer, Britain; Sardar Swaran Singh, former Foreign Minister, India; Mr John Malecela, former Foreign Minister, Tanzania. (Photo: Madan Rora)

1966–71. Archbishop Scott was Moderator of the Executive and Central Committees of the World Council of Churches 1975–83. He was made a Companion of the Order of Canada in 1978.

A Special Unit was established in the Commonwealth Secretariat to provide professional and administrative support to the Group for the duration of its work, particularly during its visits to South Africa. It drew upon resources Secretariat-wide.

A Note on the Commonwealth

The Commonwealth comprises the English-speaking world but for the United States and a few other countries. Its forty-nine sovereign member nations are located in every continent and ocean. Nearly one-third of the states of the modern international community, their populations are over a quarter of the world's people.

Uniquely in the international community outside the United Nations, the Commonwealth brings together countries at all levels of economic development. It embraces different political systems, but all its member countries acknowledge the Queen as Head of the Commonwealth.

The contemporary Commonwealth evolved out of the old British connection. Hence the different countries share both principles and practice: principles of freedom, democracy and multiracialism; practices of law, administration and education. The Commonwealth's peoples speak many languages but communicate easily through the shared language of English.

The Commonwealth's organic evolution has been matched by the growth of consultation and co-operation to meet the needs of its member countries. The modern equivalent of the old Imperial Conferences and Prime Ministers' Meetings is the biennial Commonwealth Heads of Government Meeting at which Presidents and Prime Ministers discuss issues of importance to them and the world community. Programmes of co-operation are administered by the London-based Commonwealth Secretariat set up in 1965.

The Commonwealth, an outcome of decolonization, holds self-determination as a central principle. It has long been concerned to help extend political freedoms to all the people of South Africa. In 1961 South Africa was forced to leave the Commonwealth because of its racist policies. The Commonwealth has been prominent in the world campaign against apartheid. Decisions of Commonwealth leaders led the way in the international arms embargo against South Africa and its sporting isolation through the Commonwealth's 1977 Gleneagles Agreement.

In 1985, at their summit at Nassau in the Bahamas, Commonwealth leaders decided on further pressure for change in South Africa and appointed the Commonwealth Group of Eminent Persons to promote in that country a political dialogue aimed at replacing apartheid by popular government.

The countries are: Antigua and Barbuda, Australia, The Bahamas, Bangladesh, Barbados, Belize, Botswana, Britain, Brunei Darussalam, Canada, Cyprus, Dominica, Fiji, The Gambia, Ghana, Grenada, Guyana, India, Jamaica, Kenya, Kiribati, Lesotho, Malawi, Malaysia, Maldives, Malta, Mauritius, Nauru, New Zealand, Nigeria, Papua New Guinea, St Christopher-Nevis, St Lucia, St Vincent and the Grenadines, Seychelles, Sierra Leone, Singapore, Solomon Islands, Sri Lanka, Swaziland, Tanzania, Tonga, Trinidad and Tobago, Tuvalu, Uganda, Vanuatu, Western Samoa, Zambia, Zimbabwe.

Foreword by the Commonwealth Secretary-General

Over the last six months a remarkable thing happened in one of the saddest corners of our small world. A group of seven people from five continents, black and white and brown, gave everything they had to offer – integrity, humanity, compassion, understanding and a wide experience – to holding back a darkening storm. It was remarkable most of all because, against the odds, the Commonwealth Group of Eminent Persons (a title each of them eschewed) showed, by the quality of their efforts for peaceful change in South Africa, that both change and peace are within the grasp of its people. For a brief moment, the world – and, pre-eminently, South Africans of all races – glimpsed a path of negotiation to a more worthy future.

This Report is an account of that mission to South Africa and a statement by the seven who undertook it of the realities they confronted and the perils they fear could lie ahead for all races in South Africa. It is a Report to Commonwealth leaders, but it is a testimony to all the world. It arose out of the Commonwealth Meeting in Nassau in October 1985, but it is rooted in the concern of Governments and people everywhere. Those concerns are about the inhumanities of the apartheid system and the even more terrible human suffering that lies not far ahead if a way is not found urgently to compel the dismantling of apartheid and the establishment of a non-racial representative Government in South Africa.

The message is clear: apartheid must end. It will end – if necessary, through a bloody struggle whose cost in lives may be counted in millions and whose agonies will reverberate in every corner of our multi-racial world. But it could end by peaceful means – by a genuine process of negotiation – once white South Africa accepts that the evil system by which it has sustained its dominance must end and is ready by deeds to bring it about. The Group's account shows with unique authenticity how far the Government of South Africa is from that acceptance and that readiness. It shows too that not all white South Africans stand rooted on the banks of the Rubicon; some are ready and willing to cross. And the Group's Report confirms that on the other bank those so long oppressed in South Africa, the victims of apartheid, are ready even now to join in a peaceful process of building a new South Africa in which all its people, black and white, coloured and Indian, will share in fairness and with dignity.

The Report conveys yet another message, not to South Africa but to all of us beyond it. It is a call to action, a challenge not to stand aside. The means left open to the world community are few, but they are real. Whether we call them 'sanctions' or, as the Group has done, 'economic measures', they come to the same thing: effective economic pressure, applied particularly by those major economic powers that are South Africa's principal trading partners and to which it looks for major financial flows; pressure which demands change while there is still time to bring it about by peaceful means.

When Commonwealth leaders agreed on the establishment of the Group at Nassau, they saw it as part of a programme of common action. One aspect of that programme was the set of measures against South Africa which they agreed upon as a result of their debate on sanctions. They also agreed that if, in their opinion, adequate progress had not been made towards the objectives of the Accord within six months, they would consider the adoption of further measures, and others beyond them, on a continuing and incremental basis, in order to secure the desired result within a limited period. The task of the Group was to advance the process of change in South Africa 'by all practicable means'. For the time being, at any rate, their efforts to achieve this by facilitating the process of dialogue among South Africans have been thwarted by the Government. The Group's Report makes it clear that, in the six months of their efforts, there has been no progress towards the dismantling of apartheid and the establishment of a non-racial representative Government – the essential objectives of the Accord.

The challenge that the Group's Report throws down to us all is reinforced by the circumstances in which the Government of South Africa sought to nullify this Commonwealth effort: its calculated assault on the peace process itself. The Commonwealth Group has opened up and explored the path to change. The Government of South Africa refuses to take it – indeed, would like, it seems, to seal it off. Sanctions and peace for South Africa have now become one and the same. As the Group says, even now the absence of real economic pressure on the Government – and its belief that it may never have to face such pressure – are helping to defer change. Ordinary black people throughout South Africa look to the world for more than just moral clarity. Those outside who say that sanctions will 'hurt the blacks' do not know how intense black suffering already is. It is, in any case, a judgement they have no right to make, when the blacks themselves see sanctions, and any additional suffering these involve, as preferable to the far greater tragedy they would otherwise face. This they said to the Group over and over again.

One final word; and one of hope. As this Report intimately demonstrates, the human spirit survives in South Africa in so many ways. In the courage of young children, in the churches, in the great coalition that makes up the United Democratic Front, among the women who bear some of the heaviest burdens and women's groups like Black Sash who keep faith with the spirit of caring. But, most of all, its survival is symbolized in the person of Nelson Mandela. The walls of South Africa's prisons confine him, but his spirit soars above them: a spirit of freedom, of nationalism rising above 'group', of courage and resolve that humiliates oppression; a spirit of non-racialism that looks to a democratic South Africa acknowledging black and white as fellow South Africans; a spirit that can release his entire country from bondage.

The human spirit in South Africa is crying out for the world's help, for the world's solidarity. It is proclaiming for all who allow themselves to hear that it is not freedom that white South Africa should fear but freedom's denial.

Shridath Ramphal
Marlborough House
London SW1
June 1986

COMMONWEALTH GROUP OF EMINENT PERSONS

Established pursuant to the Commonwealth Accord on Southern Africa. Nassau. October 1985

Cables: COMSECGEN LONDON SW1

Telex: 27678

Telephone: 01-839 3411

Marlborough House

Pall Mall

London SW1Y 5HX

7 June 1986

H E Mr Shridath S Ramphal
Commonwealth Secretary-General
Marlborough House
Pall Mall
LONDON SW1

Dear Secretary-General,

We forward herewith our Report and would be grateful if you could arrange to have it transmitted to Commonwealth Heads of Government.

It is not often that the chance arises to try and serve a whole country, arrest its drift to civil war, and initiate a process that might usher in a new era. We were given such a chance. If we are sad that our efforts to achieve these objectives in South Africa have been unavailing, it is not so much out of a sense of disappointment at the personal level, but acute consciousness and concern at the consequences of our failure for the future of that country.

We had fervently hoped we might succeed. Our Report in the case would have been brief. The Report which we now present is, of course, of a different character.

We have had a unique opportunity of dealing with all the parties principally concerned with events in South Africa and of visiting many of the countries of Southern Africa and talking with their leaders. In present circumstances this imposes on us a particular obligation to speak with frankness to Commonwealth leaders, indeed to the world community, of our experience and to provide with candour our assessments and our judgements.

We hope that our Report can contribute to the fulfilment of the objectives of the Nassau Accord which remains so central to the prospects for a new South Africa. It must serve not only as a record of our efforts, but as a reminder to the Commonwealth and the wider international community of the true nature of the situation in South Africa and the prospects for the future as we see them. We remain wholly convinced that those objectives Commonwealth leaders identified at Nassau must continue to be pursued through every means possible.

Members:

The Rt.Hon. MALCOLM FRASER *(Co-Chairman)* ; General OLUSEGUN OBASANJO *(Co-Chairman)*

The Rt.Hon. LORD BARBER; Dame NITA BARROW; Mr. JOHN MALECELA; Sardar SWARAN SINGH; The Most Rev. Archbishop EDWARD W. SCOTT DD.

We take some satisfaction in the fact that, despite considerable scepticism on all sides at the outset of our work, the process gradually gained the confidence of many of the parties involved and lifted the expectations of people, white and black, in South Africa (and, we believe, of people in many other countries) to new levels of hope. Such increased hope was understandable. Certainly, as we proceeded with our work, we became convinced that, not only was it a matter of the utmost urgency to dismantle apartheid and erect structures of democracy in South Africa in terms of a non-racial representative Government, but that it was essential to break the cycle of violence in the country if these objectives were to be achieved. We are convinced that all this is attainable. We deeply regret that the Government of South Africa at the end made it impossible for us to proceed further.

Throughout our work we have had the benefit of assistance by members of the Commonwealth Secretariat. The highly professional and dedicated support which they have provided has been outstanding, as has their unceasing effort over a period of considerable pressure. We are most grateful for their excellent work which has played a key part in enabling us to undertake our task. We especially wish to place on record our appreciation of the role which you, the Deputy Secretary-General, Chief Emeka Anyaoku, and the Assistant Secretary-General, Mr Moni Malhoutra, have played personally in advising and supporting us.

As you have requested, we shall hold ourselves available for the Review Meeting of Commonwealth leaders due to be held early in August.

Yours sincerely,

Malcolm Fraser

Olusegun Obasanjo

Anthony Barber

Nita Barrow

John Malecela

Swaran Singh

Edward Scott

Introduction

Our Group was appointed under the Commonwealth Accord on Southern Africa, agreed by Heads of Government in Nassau in October 1985 as a united Commonwealth response to the challenge of apartheid. The Accord in its entirety (Annex 1) provided the framework for our work; it contained both a specific injunction to the Group and a call to the South African Government to undertake five particular steps.

The South African Government was urged to declare that the system of apartheid would be dismantled and specific and meaningful action taken in fulfilment of that intent; to terminate the state of emergency; to release immediately and unconditionally Nelson Mandela and all others imprisoned or detained for their opposition to apartheid; and to establish political freedom, specifically lifting the ban on the African National Congress (ANC) and other political parties.

The fifth step – the initiation by Pretoria, in the context of a suspension of violence on all sides, of a process of dialogue with a view to establishing a non-racial and representative government – was of direct concern to the Group. It was our task to encourage, through all practical ways, the evolution of such a process of political dialogue. Naturally, that dialogue would have to be across the lines of colour, politics and religion and would have to involve the true representatives of the majority black populations – and the Accord said so.

While the first four urgent and practical steps called for by Commonwealth leaders were, in a formal sense, distinct from the assignment we were given, each was critically related to our chances of being able to facilitate a meaningful process of dialogue. Only their implementation would create the conditions, and generate the confidence, within which a genuine dialogue of change could take place.

For that reason, our Report takes each of these points in turn, commenting on them in some detail.

We were keenly aware of the limitation of time put on our mission. Once established, we had six months to do our work, in the knowledge that at the end of that period the seven Heads of Government referred to in the Accord would meet to review the situation. Having agreed a package of measures against Pretoria at the Nassau Meeting, Commonwealth Heads of Government would then consider further measures if the Review Meeting deemed progress insufficient.

There was therefore no question of the Group having anything other than a short and specific existence. This was a point we needed to stress repeatedly to those fearful that we were to be a 'Contact Group' with an indefinite life.

We were also aware that our role was limited to the task of facilitating a process of dialogue for change: for ending apartheid and establishing a genuine non-racial democracy in South Africa. It would be for those involved in that process – the representatives of all the people of South Africa – to determine the forms of change; it was not our function to prescribe what form a political settlement might take. That remained the prerogative of the South African people.

Understandable suspicions among most of the principal parties added to the difficulty and sensitivity of our mission. Among black representatives, for example, there was intense distrust of British Government policy and the intentions of the Prime Minister. The Group was wrongly perceived as being a product of the British Government's wish to resist sanctions against South Africa and a device to postpone effective international action. We therefore had a major task to establish the independence and sincerity of our undertaking.

In respect of Pretoria, Commonwealth leaders had themselves anticipated 'the possibility of initial rejection by the South African authorities' of any role for the Group. Our initial exchange of letters with the Government is at Annexes 2 and 3.

To overcome misconceptions and remove apprehensions

about the work of the Group, and to build confidence to a point from which meaningful discussions could begin, we agreed on a number of operational principles at the outset.

First, we decided that despite the considerable media interest which our work would attract, we would work quietly and in non-public ways. This meant that, while our work was in progress, we would not make any public comment or, for that matter, respond publicly to what others might say.

Second, we decided that our approach to all parties would be non-confrontational. We went to considerable lengths to create and maintain an atmosphere of cordiality. Even when severely provoked, we remained silent because of the overriding importance of the issues at stake.

Third, the Group recognized that there might be value in functioning in other ways than always as a full Group, particularly at the very beginning of the exercise, when the acceptability of the Group to all parties hung in the balance. The low-key preliminary visit to South Africa of the two Co-Chairmen, General Obasanjo and Mr Fraser, accompanied by Dame Nita Barrow, was of crucial importance in making contact, allaying suspicions, explaining our purpose and paving the way for the visit of the full Group.

In the same way, the Group sometimes chose to subdivide, to enable simultaneous visits to be made. We also, on occasion, decided to share the task of briefing the Heads of Government of neighbouring and Commonwealth countries, and other members of the international community, about the progress of the initiative. The fact that those outside South Africa who possessed some influence with one or other of the principal parties were kept fully informed enabled the Group to call upon them for assistance and support as the need arose. From time to time, that proved invaluable.

Fourth, it was important, in gaining access to all the principal parties, for the Group to demonstrate its independence. We therefore travelled alone, without any government security personnel, and accompanied only by our own small Secretariat. It was equally important to move extensively around the country, with freedom of access to all those we wished to meet, making contact with as wide a spectrum of opinion as possible, and seeing as much in the townships and elsewhere on the ground as was feasible. In this regard, we acknowledge our particular debt to Prime Minister Mulroney for making available a Canadian Air Force plane which enabled us to cover much more ground within the country than would otherwise have been possible, as well as to visit the Front-Line States.

The programme of our visits, with a list of the groups and personalities whom we met during the course of our work, is set out in Annex 4. This included a total of twenty-one meetings with Ministers of the South African Government, with leaders of political and other organizations, as well as with prominent academic, political, religious and community figures.

Only by such an intensive process of discussion was it possible for the Group to help transform an initial climate of suspicion and distrust into one where the emergence of our negotiating concept became possible.

Chapter 1
Apartheid: Dismantling or Reform?

Apartheid in Perspective

None of us was prepared for the full reality of apartheid.

As a contrivance of social engineering, it is awesome in its cruelty. It is achieved and sustained only through force, creating human misery and deprivation and blighting the lives of millions.

The degree to which apartheid has divided and compartmentalized South African society is nothing short of astounding. We understood why many visitors to South Africa could leave the country enchanted by its natural beauty and impressed by its economic achievement, yet oblivious of the scale of the human tragedy behind the façade of progress.

The living standards of South Africa's white cities and towns must rank with the highest anywhere; those of the black townships which surround them defy description in terms of 'living standards'. Apartheid creates and separates them; black and white live as strangers in the same land.

We were struck by the contrasts of residential segregation everywhere. In Cape Town, our point of arrival, we passed the black townships of Guguletu, Inyanga and Langa, the coloured townships of Athlone and the white suburbs of Mowbray and Pinelands, each at once distinctive by its physical appearance. Oddly incongruous in the centre of the city, a large area of District Six lies fallow. Once a coloured and Indian area, it is idle but for a few churches and mosques and some new government buildings. A decade has passed since its vibrant Indian and coloured communities, living harmoniously as neighbours, were forcibly removed, many to the Cape Flats up to 40 kilometres away. Lamp posts on empty streets stand as witnesses to the agonies of that removal. But memories are

Service Station at Hanover – whose toilets are still segregated. Some 'Eminents' noticed too late! (Photo: Jeremy Pope)

deeply etched into the conscience of Capetoneans of all races, and private developers contemplating the redevelopment of District Six have counted the consequences in public wrath and have not proceeded.

Crossroads, on the outskirts of Cape Town, is in many ways a symbol of the apartheid system. Here, in defiance of the 'homelands' policy and the Group Areas Act and of persistent attempts to remove them forcibly to their allotted areas, thousands of families have chosen to squat. When we visited in March the community, despite severe hardship, was sticking together. Its families were crowded into crude shanties, fashioned from discarded sheets of corrugated iron and lined with cardboard and polythene in an attempt to keep out the cold. The shanties have neither sewage system nor electricity and are serviced only by a few communal water taps. Yet, in a triumph of the human spirit, the people were clean, the shacks generally tidy.

Even in conditions such as these the infant mortality rate, we were told, is barely a quarter of that in the 'homelands': a telling commentary on the degree of deprivation there. Indeed, the almost total absence of employment opportunities in the 'homelands' is one of the factors forcing families into Crossroads. Another is, of course, the possibility of their being together as families, even in these squalid conditions.

Beyond Crossroads, we saw for ourselves the state of overcrowded (and much of it ramshackle) black urban housing – in townships such as Johannesburg's Soweto, where perhaps almost 2 million people were living in housing designed for 800,000; the squalor of Port Elizabeth's Soweto, built on what resembles a rubbish dump; the conditions in Durban's Kwa Mashu, in Johannesburg's Alexandra, in Pretoria's Mamelodi.

By contrast, most white suburbs were pictures of affluence, well away from the sights and sounds of black townships. For the greater part, whites are able to go about their daily lives without any direct exposure to the conditions in the townships.

We were sought out by squatters from the Cape Town suburb of Hout Bay, blacks continuing to live in the mixed black/coloured townships where they had been born, resisting continuing attempts to move them to the solely black township of Khayelitsha on the windswept Cape Flats. Not only do they wish to remain in the community they regard as home, but their R.300 per month income would be consumed almost entirely by the cost of commuting: removal to Khayelitsha would effectively result in their becoming unemployed.

The pattern of segregation we first witnessed in Cape Town was even more stark away from the city. In the Karoo each pleasant white farming centre has its own satellite black and coloured township, squalid reservoirs quarantined from white areas but from which they draw labour. The neat white town of Cradock has its swimming pool; in the neighbouring black township of Lingelihle children have only a cesspit in which to play and keep cool. This story was frequently repeated – throughout the Midlands, in the Eastern Cape, on the outskirts of Port Elizabeth and in the commuter belts of Johannesburg and Pretoria. Indeed, as we drove around the country it quickly became apparent that whether in urban areas or in the countryside, we would be able to tell, without ever seeing a single inhabitant, in which group's 'area' we were – so stark are the Government-ordained disparities.

Despite economic and social disparities of long-standing and elements of racial discrimination, South Africa was not always like this. However, when in 1948 the incoming National Party Government, controlled by the Afrikaners, embarked on its systematic programme of apartheid, the Group Areas Act was passed. Under this law, urban blacks, coloureds, Indians and whites, already segregated to some degree, were all to be compelled to live in their 'own' areas – areas designated by the State.

To make the Group Areas Act effective it is, of course, first necessary to classify each and every individual. This is provided for in the Population Registration Act, a rigid system based on appearance, general acceptance and descent, which divides up the population first into black, white and coloured. The coloured grouping is then subdivided into Cape coloured, Cape Malay, Griqua, Indian, Chinese, 'other Asiatic' and 'other coloured'. Blacks now form ten 'national units', each with its 'reserve'. Thus has the so-called 'nation of minorities' been fashioned by government fiat. Whites alone, despite their linguistic, historical and cultural differences, are spared such sub-classification.

The 'reserves', the areas to which, under legislation of 1913 and 1936, blacks were restricted if they wished to buy additional land, have a long history. They were, however, used by the architects of apartheid not only to create the so-called 'homelands' but as the basis of a more formal and enduring division of the country, giving some 86.3 per cent of its land to whites and a meagre 13.7 per cent to about six times as many blacks. The 86.3 per cent becomes a 'white' country, a white South Africa; the 13.7 per cent was to be fragmented into ten 'self-governing homelands' for the blacks, each destined to achieve 'independence'. Thus, a predominantly black country becomes predominantly white, and the black becomes an alien in his own land. More than this, each black was assigned to a particular part of the country according to his tribal origin, language and culture, even though these distinctions had faded with the move to the cities. That this approach was at best haphazard is illustrated by the number of 'homelands'. Various numbers were considered. Simply to have two, based on the Sotho and Nguni linguistic groupings, would have been to create artificial 'states' so large that they might one day rebound on their makers. Enough were needed to diffuse power sufficiently. Eight were established: subsequently this became ten. The 'homelands' ' lack of geographical unity gives the lie to any basis in history. One 'homeland', KwaZulu, is now a jumble of some ten jigsaw pieces – an archipelagic 'state' scattered across a continental white 'sea'. Lebowa and Bophuthatswana each have six such distinct 'island' areas. In 1972, before more recent consolidations were made. KwaZulu had as many as twenty-nine separate island blocks; the Ciskei and Bophuthatswana each had nineteen.

Those living outside the areas designated for them were moved – voluntarily if they agreed, forcibly if they did not. Whites were not exempted, and thousands were relocated. But overwhelmingly the burden fell on blacks, millions of whom were moved, often to be dumped without compensation in distant, arid areas designated as their 'homelands'. If not with quite the same crudeness of former years, the system of removals continues today, even as the Government asserts that apartheid is dead.

Progressively as the 'homelands' moved to 'independence', blacks would be stripped of their South African citizenship, would have, instead, the citizenship of a new, 'independent homeland state' and require visas to enter 'white' South Africa, other than for short periods. As of 1986, four 'homelands' have been accorded 'independence' – Transkei, Bophuthatswana, Ciskei and Venda. KwaNdebele is due to become the fifth, on 11 December 1986.

Within this concept the coloureds and Indians both presented difficulty. The strategy had to concede that the former had not even a fictitious 'homeland'. It also eventually had to concede the self-evident fact that the Indian population was a permanent feature of the country, even if during the first decade of apartheid its eventual 'return' to India was confidently asserted. However, the whites outnumbered both groups combined.

We did not formally visit the 'independent homelands', none of which is recognized internationally. In our travels criss-crossing the country, however, it was impossible not to enter 'homeland' territory. We therefore had occasion to observe the circumstances of these 'homelands', among them the Transkei, Lebowa, KwaNdebele and KwaZulu. We saw the primitive conditions under which people live, prevented over the years by the pass laws from seeking work in urban areas, and families from joining menfolk there. (The pass laws are now being replaced by 'orderly urbanization', which we discuss later.) We were told of the many who daily make the arduous bus trip between home and white workplace, a heavily subsidized journey of up to four or five hours each way. In the economics of apartheid, the Government prefers the high cost of subsidizing such travel to having more blacks live in the urban areas.

Those in work too far distant to commute, and who have not been granted 'residence rights', often live in the cities for eleven months of the year in 'single men's quarters' – a euphemism for crowded huts with amenities devoid of any semblance of privacy and violating the most basic norms of human

Communal facilities, single men's hostel, Soweto. (Photo: Malcolm Fraser)

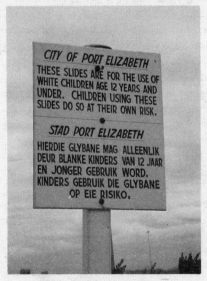

(Photo: Malcolm Fraser)

Crowded men's hostel, Soweto. (Photo: Malcolm Fraser)

Farm labourer, wife and child born by the roadside in the Karoo Desert. He
had been summarily dismissed. Farm workers receive little legal protection.
(Photo: Hugh Craft)

decency. We were reminded by Ministers and white businessmen that there are worse slums in other parts of the world. 'Here, there is a First World and a Third World,' we were told. 'Do not judge the Third World by First World standards.' Yet this is to ignore the calculated creation and maintenance of these different worlds in one country, and the determination that the demands of the First World should be met at the expense of the Third. There is abysmal poverty elsewhere in the world, but nowhere is it institutionalized as in South Africa and with as little prospect for its victims to escape the poverty trap.

The apartheid system not only sustains white political dominance; it is equally designed to keep blacks economically weak and confined to low-paid jobs. It excludes blacks from significant ownership of land, severely restricts their business opportunity and ensures cheap labour for white-owned industry, farming and commerce.

The 'homelands' are in reality rural slums, reservoirs of labour for the 'white areas' where more than four-fifths of economic activity is located. Educational provision and employment policy have been equally discriminatory. Blacks do not have equal access to jobs; despite the recent abolition of job reservation laws, inadequate opportunities for education and training and informal bars against black employment maintain white dominance in all white-collar occupations. Further, blacks are paid much less than whites for the same jobs. Average black earnings, as a result of both job and pay discrimination, are less than a quarter of white earnings. Whites – about 15 per cent of the population – are estimated to have received nearly 60 per cent of total personal disposable income in 1984, blacks less than 30 per cent. Some estimates put black unemployment at more than 3 million in a labour force of 7 to 8 million.

In a virtual extension of the 'homelands' policy, South Africa has succeeded in converting the economies of neighbouring countries like Lesotho and Botswana into preserves of labour for its mines and farms. Notwithstanding high unemployment among South Africa's own blacks, it employs some 350,000 workers from neighbouring states as legal migrants with perhaps up to a million others as illegal migrants. This pool of foreign labour helps the South African economy by depressing the general wage level, and the Government to maintain control over the labour force.

The Government points to these workers as demonstrating that conditions in South Africa are not as bad as portrayed. But the fact is that attempts by neighbouring states to improve their economies and reduce dependency on South Africa have been continuously thwarted by South African economic pressure and military sabotage; South Africa sees in their dependency a measure of political insurance for itself.

In marked contrast to earlier occasions, recent unrest in South Africa has not been confined to the urban areas. It has reached into the white countryside and engulfed the black 'homelands'. Even in an area previously as calm as Bophuthatswana, the measure of consent with which the local administration once governed has now been withdrawn, violence has flared and paratroopers have been used in attempts to restore order. We can understand the blacks' perception of the 'homelands' as very much part of the apartheid system and the claim that the 'homeland' leaders are increasingly both beneficiaries and upholders of that system.

We visited Moutse, an area some 140 kilometres to the north-east of Johannesburg now being compulsorily annexed from 'white' South Africa to be made part of the improverished 'homeland' of KwaNdebele. Not only is this manifestly against the will of Moutse's 120,000 inhabitants, many of whom saw in us a chance to avoid this fate, but they told us that they bear no cultural affinity whatever with the Ndebele. They regarded their area as being offered to the rulers of KwaNdebele – whose 'vigilantes', they claimed, regularly terrorize Moutse's helpless inhabitants – as a reward for their taking 'independence'.

For apartheid to end, the 'homelands' policy must be abandoned. Yet even while we were there, the Government reaffirmed that 'independence' will be granted to KwaNdebele before the year's end.

One area where change was most manifest, is that of public amenities. When we first arrived the hotels we used were simply designated 'international' as an exception to apartheid's segregation of facilities. Latterly all hotels have been exempted and are now allowed to admit people of all races as residents or as casual patrons of their restaurants and bars. Cinemas are increasingly being desegregated, and the white beach at Port Elizabeth, on whose sands our Co-Chairmen walked amidst controversy, is now open to all. True, segregation signs are still to be seen in many areas – even on toilets in service stations. In some centres, too, economic forces have not yet dictated the desegregation of public transport. But, by and large, public parks, libraries and a host of other facilities are now open to all. However, in numerous establishments the reservation of the right of admission – a euphemism for racial discrimination – remains.

There have been other changes. There is increasing desegregation in the work place. Some reforms, however, are halfhearted. The Mixed Marriages Act has been repealed, and life for a few hundred a year has noticeably brightened, but this still involves a racial reclassification in terms of the Group Areas Act. For example, a white who marries a coloured must move to a coloured township.

And so the question remains: does all this make any real difference to the impact of apartheid on the lives of blacks? In a country where the blacks are so poor, where white incomes per capita are ten times those of black and where the responsibilities of the extended family system place a heavy burden on any black in work, those blacks rich enough to dine at Johannesburg's Carlton Hotel or Durban's Maharani are very few in number. And even they, when the meal is over, must return to their designated township. To the casual visitor, apartheid may appear to be on the way out. In its essential elements, it remains very much intact.

In our travels we were also struck by the elegant buildings and manicured grounds of schools in white areas. These contrasted starkly with the shabby buildings, unkempt grounds and high perimeter fences of schools in black townships. Often there were new steel posts along these fence lines, bent askew by black students convinced that the authorities planned to use them to electrify the fences. We found no evidence that this was the case, but their belief illustrates the degree to which communication has collapsed between the authorities and black students. Simply for us to see the disparities between the two types of facilities was more graphic than any statistics. These show that despite recent increases on black education, the Government spends seven times as much on a white child as on a black, and that many black students drop out of school because their parents cannot afford the seemingly modest fees.

In the evolution of apartheid it was important that blacks should not be over-educated. In 'white' South Africa they were to have a role subservient to whites. Thus education was deliberately withheld to ensure that blacks would not be educated to a level where they would aspire to positions in white society from which they were excluded. As part of this policy mission schools, which had hitherto provided education of a high standard for some blacks, were forced to close. 'Bantu' education was entrusted to the Native Affairs Department rather than the Department of Education, and predominantly white universities that had previously admitted blacks were now prohibited from doing so. Instead, a series of separate inferior universities and 'tribal' colleages were established.

In the Government's scheme for ending apartheid, Ministers assured us that separate education was to remain. It is an 'own affair', a 'non-negotiable'.

There has, none the less, been a qualitative change in black education which itself fuels the present unrest. As the South African economy has diversified from agriculture and minerals extraction, so the need has grown for a more skilled and mobile black workforce. The Government's response in upgrading levels of black education in recent years – though still far from adequately – has given rise to a generation of students less ready to accept the imposition of apartheid with apathy.

Yet, if apartheid is very much a system designed to serve the whites, it is also an extremely wasteful one. The sheer bureaucracy required to sustain its machinery is vast; the commitment of resources to security for the maintenance of apartheid is massive; a leading economist informed us that

Civil Service salaries account for two-thirds of budget expenditure.

Time and again, as we travelled, looked, listened and talked, the exploitative nature of apartheid was forcefully brought home to us. So too the fact that blacks generally are no longer prepared to tolerate either exploitation or gross disparity. There have been waves of protest in the past, invariably put down by the security forces. Today's is without precedent in its scale and intensity. In protest at housing conditions, rent offices have been ransacked and stand, roofless and windowless, in townships where arrears of rent now run into many millions of rand. In frustration at those who have aided the system by joining Government-backed 'town councils', 'collaborators' have been hounded out of office – frequently out of house and home and often 'necklaced' – as angry black residents have vented their fury and assumed responsibility for their own affairs. We saw for ourselves 'collaborators', like members of a leper colony exorcised from the township, living in army tents and under armed guard, at the small rural town of Hanover; elsewhere, others were enclosed behind high wire-meshed fences.

Students have often been on strike over educational issues; schools have been burnt down and destroyed and teachers paid to do nothing. Calls for work stay-aways, consumer boycotts and general strikes achieve a level of response and a solidarity that could not have been dreamt of even five years ago. The dependence of white-owned shops on black purchasing power has been brought home to the white community as never before.

The Government has now been driven to the point where it is unable to police its own laws in some black and coloured townships, where its policies inevitably lead to systematic repression by the security forces. This is paralleled by violent, vigilante action by favoured blacks against people rebelling against apartheid and forcing the pace for a democratic South Africa. There is a widespread belief among black groups and some white elements, like Black Sash, that such action receives active support from the Government.

We deal later in our Report with the all-pervading atmosphere of repression, and of townships encircled by armoured personnel carriers, whose occupants did not hesitate to menace even us with their weapons.

Yet after constant and recurring cycles of repression, black resistance has not only been maintained it has been strengthened and made more resolute. Catalysed in particular by opposition to the Tricameral Parliament, it has resolved into a new and telling strategy for change: to make South Africa ungovernable and apartheid unworkable.

The Government's Programme

In recent years changes have been taking place within South Africa. For whites who have grown up in a rigorous apartheid society, these changes appear to be both major and meaningful. It is necessary to examine these, and other changes fore-shadowed by the Government, to assess the direction in which the Government is taking the country. We seek not to enumerate all the details of the Government's programme but rather to describe its underlying philosophy.

As we saw for ourselves, visible changes have indeed taken place. In addition to those already noted, increasing numbers of blacks are being permitted to purchase freehold (if only in black townships). 'Free-trade areas' open to all races have been established in some cities. Black trade unions have been recognized. A uniform identity document is being provided for all population groups, and if blacks will still be fingerprinted on reaching age 16, so too in future will all other sections of the community. In these and other respects, various discriminatory laws have been repealed or are being phased out. However, it needs to be borne in mind that in South Africa there is a multiplicity of laws affecting race.

For the blacks, the great majority of the people of South Africa, the most significant reform since apartheid was introduced has been the move to abolish the 'pass', the hated 'dompas'. For generations the 'pass' (which historically dates from 1809) has been an ever-present manifestation to the black of his bondage. Without it, he could not work or be in an urban area; failure to produce it upon demand resulted in immediate arrest. It was very much his 'book of life'.

Now the hated 'pass' is to go; those imprisoned for 'pass'-law offences have been released. Yet it is illuminating to note that the abolition of a document symbolic of more human misery than any other aspect of apartheid's administration has evoked no sense of freedom among blacks. More than anything else, this mute black reaction demonstrated to us the current acute lack of trust. The abolition of the 'pass' – the cause for which sixty-nine people died at Sharpeville in 1960, for which Chief Albert Luthuli was banished, and for which in part the African National Congress (ANC) and the Pan-Africanist Congress of Azania (PAC) were banned – has evoked at best scepticism, at worst indifference.

That blacks have cause for scepticism is manifest from this being the second occasion upon which the 'pass' has been re-scinded. As long ago as 1952 the Bantu (Abolition of Passes and Co-ordination of Documents) Act purported to abolish the 'pass' but substituted the 'registration book'. Blacks understandably now wait to see whether in practice the 'common identity document' will bring change or will simply be another exercise in 'change without change'. We note that the identification numbers assigned to people under the Population Registration Act, which code them according to race, are carried forward into the new arrangements.

Our discussions suggest that the pending abolition of 'influx control' will lift a burden from many blacks at present illegally in urban areas and free them to find employment and add their names to (already over-lengthy) housing waiting lists. It could also introduce a new element of mobility. Blacks who are not treated as 'foreigners' (whether by reason of their being from outside the country or as a consequence of the 'independence' of their particular 'homeland') should be free to move to seek employment or to be joined by their families.

However, because the townships are heavily overcrowded and the Government is intent on maintaining racial segregation, the promised new mobility is likely to be heavily circumscribed. Indications of this are already apparent in the Government's

White Paper on 'orderly urbanization'. Wide ministerial powers are now being given to deal with squatters and hefty penalties imposed on the owners and occupiers of land where squatters establish themselves. In the total picture, acute housing shortages in all urban areas, stringent enforcement of town planning and health requirements (already foreshadowed) and perpetuation of the Group Areas Act (which confines urban blacks to minute and crowded areas of land) are likely to endure for some considerable time to come. All this will ensure that not only will the white-feared 'black invasion' from rural areas not take place but also that men separated from their families will not be joined by them. The hailed new 'freedom of movement' may in large part be illusory. However, because the new 'common identify document' does not, in the precise terms of the Bill, have to be carried at all times and produced upon demand, the new arrangement, properly administered, does afford some chance that relationships between police and the black community may ease, at least in this area of law enforcement.

Yet the question central to any discussion of the Government's programme of reform is whether or not apartheid is to end. The removal of one of apartheid's manifestations – the 'pass' – is not in itself conclusive if the fundamental controls over the lives of blacks are to remain.

The Government has used various descriptions in respect of apartheid – that it is 'outmoded', 'ended' or even 'dead'. As blacks repeatedly pointed out to us, the South African Government practises a form of 'government by semantics'. What, then, does the Government mean when it refers to apartheid in this way?

The Government provided us with a definition in the following words:

If by apartheid is meant:
● political domination by any one community of any other;
● the exclusion of any community from the political decision-making process;
● injustice or inequality in the opportunities available for any community;
● racial discrimination and impairment of human dignity;

the South African Government rejects that concept and is committed to the dismantling of that system.

The South African Government is committed to reform aimed at the realization of a democratic political system for all the communities of the country. It is the Government's viewpoint that only democractic institutions can meet the demands of justice and fairness.

The South African Government is committed to the removal of discrimination, not only from the statute books but also from South African society as a whole.

The definition only partially eases our task in answering the question, for it is deceptively misleading, particularly in its references to 'decision-making', 'inequality' and 'discrimination'. It must be read with numerous other pronouncements of government policy, including those of the State President and Ministers. These include assertions of a 'right of self-determination for minorities', which the Government in discussions with us clearly sees as embracing separate residential, educational and health facilities. The constant theme is one of 'group rights' at the expense of individual rights and freedoms. In the State President's words, the Government is 'prepared to share its decision-making power **with other communities**'; he foresees 'participation **by all communities**', the sharing of power between **these communities**'. In its unambiguous insistence on a political structure based on communities, the Government is in reality seeking to preserve and entrench a society based on racial groups. While in any ordinary circumstances a requirement that 'there is no domination of one population group over another' might seem reasonable, in the circumstances of South Africa these words have quite a different meaning. Indeed, the State President has specifically ruled out 'the principle of one man one vote in a unitary system'. But more than this: it is the clear intention of the Government that, in whatever constitutional structures that ultimately emerge, each 'group' will hold some form of veto over government decisions affecting it. This would enable whites to prevent the economic and social restructuring of South Africa that is essential if the legacy of four decades of apartheid – and three hundred years of discrimination – is to be remedied.

The concept of white domination – of power-sharing without losing white control – is enshrined in the present Tricameral Constitution under which whites, coloureds and Indians are given their own parliamentary chambers, with some power over their 'own affairs'. Not so blacks, responsibility for whose 'own affairs' is vested in the State President.

The way in which the new Constitution is framed is also instructive, as the Government claims that this introduced 'power-sharing' among the groups concerned. Yet, stripped to its barest essentials, no legislation of any consequence can be enacted without at least white acquiescence. Neither of the other groups holds this power of veto.

The white veto is achieved by having the composition of various joint committees reflect the sizes of the respective racial groups. As, in terms of aboslute numbers, whites outnumber Indians and coloureds combined, so too can they outvote them all on such bodies as the electoral college (which elects the State President) and the President's Council (which by a simple majority breaks any deadlock occurring as a result of legislation not being passed in all three 'houses'). These arrangements do not apply to blacks. Were they to do so, the whites would lose the numerical superiority they now insist upon for themselves.

The Constitution, when proposed in 1983, was to go to a referendum. It was endorsed comfortably by whites: liberal whites and those of the far right united in opposition. But such was the hostility to it among all other sections of the community – and not just blacks – that the Government abandoned planned referenda of Indian and coloured voters. Instead it simply imposed the Constitution on the country at large through the existing Parliament. And, from its viewpoint, wisely so. For in the subsequent election to the coloured and Indian 'houses', up to 80 per cent or more of the eligible voters abstained. Those who stood for election now found themselves rejected by many of their own people and, to a large measure, captives of a system many of them had campaigned against over the years with considerable fortitude. The boycott by coloured and Indian voters was so dramatic that it can be seen only as a resounding rejection of the Government's programme by those intended to be its prime beneficiaries.

The Government has sought consistently to dictate both the content and the pace of change. Its approach seeks not to unify the country but to divide and entrench each of its several communities, locking each group into its own economy (although with an element of 'free trade') and limiting economic advancement in the main to the resources available within, and generated by, the group in question. It is an approach which seeks to preserve the whites in their position of political and economic privilege and domination.

To date, the Government's approach to power-sharing has been cast within the parameters of apartheid and with the backstop of a white veto. Out task was to encourage the Government to adopt a genuine approach to power-sharing: an approach which accepted the ending of apartheid and sought a negotiated settlement under which a non-racial and truly representative government would be established, and the legitimate rights of minorities protected. While future constitutional arrangements are not a matter for us, we wholly accept that these should provide adequate and appropriate safeguards and guarantees for minorities. But, of course, anything in the nature of a general and permanent 'group veto' would be totally unacceptable to the black people.

Nor has the Government limited its 'group' approach to government at the national level. Even while we were in the country it was pressing forward with a wholesale reconstruction of Provincial Government built around assigning 'own affairs' matters to the respective parliamentary 'houses' and establishing government-appointed boards to manage common utilities. It was in this context, too, that black 'town councils' were established in the past, with responsibility for housing and the duty to find finance from within their impoverished communities to fund it. The consequential rises in rent have been one of the causes of the present unrest.

The 'group' approach is also enshrined in the Government's proposed 'National Council'. The State President, in January, declared his intention to 'negotiate' the establishment of such a body on an interim basis. The style in which these 'negotiations' have been conducted is instructive, for there has been no discernible attempt whatever to discuss the matter with the principal representatives of black opinion. Nor, indeed, would we have expected any of them to allow themselves to be co-opted into the Tricameral Constitution in this or any other way.

Instead a Bill has now been published to provide a vehicle for discussing a new constitution and to give blacks a say in the process of government 'affecting their interests'. Ostensibly the Bill is the product of negotiation. In reality it simply presses ahead with the Government's own plans for the country's future, without the benefit of any significant consultation and agreement. However, it was suggested to us informally that there could be other forums for negotiations.

The Council, as proposed, is to include leaders of all communities, the leaders of non-independent 'homelands' and 'at least' ten urban black leaders among them. However, as in all such councils and committees, the State President, through his power of appointment, retains control.

It is, in the circumstances, unlikely to achieve 'more national unity', as the Government hopes.

In our view the various reforms undertaken or foreshadowed to date must be viewed against the background of a determination not to give up white control. The harshness of apartheid, in many of its manifestations, has been and is being softened. But the essential pillars remain: the 'homelands' policy, the Population Registration Act, the Group Areas Act. Not only do they remain, but the 'homelands' policy is being further developed: KwaNdebele is to acquire a notional 'independence' in December, and those to regain citizenship under the Government's 1986 legislative programme do not appear to include those who were deprived of it and are now living in the 'homelands'.

The abolition of the 'homelands' policy would mark the beginning of the end of the policy of a white South Africa. From a legal point of view, this could be achieved without difficulty; the only barrier is political will.

We would see little difficulty in an immediate repeal of the Group Areas Act, which we note is presently under a study by a Government Commission. In some areas it is already ineffective, such as in the Johannesburg suburb of Hillbrow and in parts of Durban, where non-whites have, through companies and through white nominees, purchased property in white areas. In other areas it has never been imposed, such as in the Cape Town suburb of Observatory, where people of all races live together. If the Act were removed, any change in racial mix would still be very gradual. Certainly, it would not provoke the 'revolutionary chaos' against which the State President has cautioned. Indeed, if all apartheid laws were to be repealed, economic factors alone would militate against dramatic change for a long time.

The Government rejects all Western constitutional models, and we do not criticize them for arguing that any constitution should not be imported from abroad but should reflect the needs and aspirations of the people within. However, the libraries of South African universities are crowded with academic writings, and constitutional models in an industrious but vain search for a solution – both workable and likely to be acceptable to the people at large – in which 'group rights' would be preserved. The 'KwaNatal' discussions presently proceeding in Durban represent the latest attempt in exploring such a solution. It is, we repeat, not for us to dictate what may or may not be acceptable to all the people of South Africa but simply to observe that, in our considered view, peace will never come to South Africa until such time as its constitutional structures have as their foundation the consent of the governed: not that of minorities, not that of groups, but that of the people as a whole.

In terms of the Nassau Accord we have asked ourselves these questions: Has the South African Government declared that the system of apartheid will be dismantled, and has it taken specific and meaningful action in fufilment of that intent?

Recognizing that, to a specially high degree in South Africa, actions speak louder than words, we are sceptical of the intention of the Government to dismantle completely the system of apartheid in the sense that that system is known and understood the world over. Their actions up to this point do not justify any claim that apartheid is being dismantled. The argument that the

considerable change which we have seen is directed to that end founders, irretrievably, on the rocks of 'group rights' and white control.

Attitudes Among the White Community

We recognize the huge difficulties of adjustment facing the white community. As the editor of one leading English daily put it recently: 'It will not be easy for many whites to settle down to what is their inevitable destiny in a multiracial country where the population is three-quarters black'.

There was thus, we sensed, a widely felt need for distractions within the white community. The passion for sport, especially rugby, provided such an opportunity. On the arrival of a 'rebel' New Zealand rugby team, a Rugby Board official was reported as exulting that rugby had 'changed the face of South Africa' by driving Nelson Mandela from the front page on to page six. As 'white' South Africa basked in the illusion of an imagined international respectability, the death toll continued to mount unabated in the townships and in the 'homelands'. The response of whites to the presence of overseas sportsmen – whether representative or not – brought home to us the impact and importance of the international sports boycott of which the Gleneagles Agreement is a vital part. The lengths to which the South African authorities are prepared to go in elevating the importance of visiting teams, and the huge financial inducements they offer, reveal their craving for supposed international recognition. That alone demonstrates the continuing need for this form of pressure, including the strict observance of the Gleneagles Agreement.

Of course, big business has for some years favoured reform. Needing a more skilled and mobile labour force to service South African industry as the economy has moved away from a simple dependence on mining and agriculture, business has called for increased spending on education, better housing and the abolition of influx control.

Through the Urban Foundation a number of businesses have

contributed to black home-ownership schemes and have moved to provide amenities in the townships which would otherwise be lacking. The recent visit of several prominent businessmen to Lusaka to meet the ANC is testimony of their clear appreciation of the need for a negotiated settlement.

Some white opinion has opposed apartheid from the very beginning, most notably the woman's organization Black Sash. Added to this are the very many organizations and individuals who have been active – indeed, courageous – in combating apartheid in its many manifestations.

Newer sections of the white community have come to embrace the need for change, including, during the course of our visit, a leading group of white students from the academic heartland of Afrikanerdom, the University of Stellenbosch. Their call for negotiaitons with the ANC and the release of Nelson Mandela was indeed an encouraging sign.

Clearly, a number of Afrikaners, including some who trace their roots back over three hundred years to the original Dutch Colony, feel their whole future threatened and see no country which might match up to their 'fatherland'. Some of them are turning to the misguided notion that their power to subdue blacks by using the full power of the security forces renders them sufficiently strong to resist fundamental change. They close their eyes to the simple fact, acknowledged by Government and business alike, that both whites and blacks separately have it within their power to destroy the country.

Thus in recent months the country has witnessed the emergence of a growing and increasingly assertive extreme right wing as Afrikanerdom begins to fragment under the cumulative weight of the pressures we have described. This phenomenon is not altogether surprising. For two generations, whites in South Africa have lived as beneficiaries of apartheid in a system engineered by a political party which constantly asserted white supremacy. When they witness an apparent change in Government theology, with the rhetoric of total white control giving way to talk of power-sharing, a backlash of some description is inevitable. But just as the far right is a creation of the National Party, so too must it accept responsibility for dealing with it. The need for courageous leadership has never been greater. Certainly, whatever the threat from the extreme right, the Government can still rely on carrying the majority of the white community if it takes bold decisions to bring peace and prosperity to the country as a whole.

Inded there is a growing number of whites, a number of whom we met, who are 'ahead' of the Government and see the peaceful eradication of apartheid as the only hope. Our impression in this regard is also borne out by a number of recent opinion polls. Dr Alex Boraine, in his speech of resignation in Parliament just before our first visit to South Africa, called on those he knew to be in the ruling National Party and discontented with the Government's progress towards reform to stand up and be counted.

Nevertheless, it remains the case that many whites genuinely entertain fears about their future in any new dispensation. We found a keen awareness of this among responsible black leaders, together with an acknowledgement of the need to allay them.

It is a tragedy that the Government, as a matter of policy, is seeking to deepen these fears. A picture has deliberately been built up of the ANC as an organization dominated by communists and wedded to creating a Marxist State in South Africa. Early in June the Government, in a mass publicity booklet entitled *Talking with the ANC*, insinuated that Nelson Mandela himself is a communist and that twenty-three out of thirty members of the ANC's National Executive are either members or active supporters of the South African Communist Party.

More detached analysts dispute these figures (which we note are even higher than those given to us by the Government just three weeks ago) and question the picture that is frequently presented by Pretoria of the ANC as a component of international communism, dedicated to the pursuit of revolutionary power. Tom Lodge, for example, one of South Africa's foremost experts on the internal politics of the ANC, regards the Government's figures, and its view of the extent of communist influence in the ANC, as very considerable exaggerations. In his assessment, the ANC is essentially 'a movement of pragmatists, not ideologues'. Its commitment to changing South

Africa's present apartheid-based social, economic and political arrangements 'stems not from the logic of an externally derived Marxist revolutionary conspiracy, as is so often asserted by the apologists for the present order. It comes rather from a popular political tradition of which the ANC is a central component. The ANC's radicalism is a reflection of the times and the society that have produced it. It is an indigenous force and an inescapable part of the political reality of this country.'

Everything we have learned is consistent with this assessment.

Chapter 2

The Issue of Violence

Throughout our work in South Africa, the issue of violence cropped up again and again. It is, in a way, central to the political debate in the country. The Government demands of its opponents a renunciation of violence – or a 'commitment to non-violence' – as a precondition to negotiation; its opponents say their violence is reactive, and call upon the Government to abandon its violence first. Where does the truth lie?

All Governments have coercive powers, and regard the maintenance of law and order as their first duty. If the Government of South Africa was a democratic government, its claims in this regard would command some respect. But the situation in South Africa is different; the objectives of the South African Government are different; and the rules and conventions governing the use of state power are different. It is important that these differences should be clearly understood if the issue of violence is to be viewed in proper perspective.

The Apartheid State: Origins of Violence

The grand design of apartheid, as conceived by the Nationalists in 1948, was to make South Africa a 'white' country. It was for this reason, as we have already mentioned, that nearly seven-eighths of the territory was to be and still is, exclusively for the small white minority (now about 4.8 million people) and the remainder for the overwhelming black majority (now over 24 million people). The implementation of this design over the years, with the Government riding rough-shod over the wishes and traditions of the people affected, necessitated coercion by the State in a manner and on a scale which reveal the inherent violence of the system.

The making of 'white' South Africa required a number of constitutional changes.

First, non-whites enfranchised under the 1910 Union had to lose the vote. This was achieved, in the face of strenuous opposition, by the Government packing the Senate and so subverting a Supreme Court judgment.

Second, because the Afrikaner wanted to believe that he was acting from convictions of righteousness, a number of fictions had to be created. The first was to the effect that blacks were not South African at all: rather, they belong to one or another of the 'homelands', according to their tribal origins, language or culture, even though there had been much inter-marriage and fading of tribal roots with the move to the cities.

As a consequence, to date some 8 million blacks have been stripped of their South African citizenship to become, in the South African legal system, foreigners in their own land. Carried to its conclusion, all blacks would become citizens of other lands, and whites would comprise the overwhelming majority in a 'white' South Africa. Recently, however, this approach has been modified to the extent that citizens of 'homelands' who live permanently in 'white' South Africa may have their South African citizenship restored. About 3 million blacks stand to benefit.

The strategy also called for stringent control of the movement of the black population. There was thus a clamp-down in the cities. Thousands of blacks, technically there illegally, were rounded up and trucked off to the 'reserves'. As those whose labour was needed in the urban areas were now seen as 'temporary visitors', townships designated for blacks were systematically run down.

Some concession was made for those who had been in continuous employment for lengthy periods, but for the rest the era of forced removals was to begin. The exact total displaced in this way may never be known, but in 1983 the Surplus People Project estimated that between 1960 and 1983 a total of 3,522,900 removals had taken place, and at least a further 1.8

Devastation at the Indian school at Phoenix settlement, near Durban. (Photo: Jeremy Pope)

million were under threat of removal. Of these, three-quarters were black and most of the rest (resited under the Group Areas Act) were coloured and Indian. Only 2,262 white families were removed under the Group Areas Act. These removals, which continue to the present day, were achieved with a callousness that has shocked the world. Families were uprooted from areas where they and their forbears had lived for generations, trucked in some instances for hundreds of miles and dumped in arid, uninviting areas with the barest amenities, if any.

Even the Government was compelled to admit that there was an 'element of force in some removals', having previously claimed that they were carried out only with 'compassion and respect for human dignity'. Spokesmen insist that removals today are voluntary – although we heard from people that they were being given the stark alternative to consent or be arrested.

Nor was consideration given to the deep traditional roots the blacks had with the land where they had long been settled but which fell outside the designated 'homelands'. In most societies, considerable spiritual significance is attached to land and to the burial grounds of previous generations. In this the blacks are no exception, but there was no place for sensitivity to be shown if a 'white' South Africa were to be achieved. Nor was there adequate (or, at times, any) compensation for those dispossessed of property or of the ability to farm. In bringing about a 'white' South Africa, the losses must lie where they fell.

But having achieved a segregation of the land in this way, the 'white' urban areas still required labour. This was supplied by attaching the fictional label of 'migrant worker' to a person from a 'homeland' who came into 'white' South Africa – without his family – to service the needs of whites and of white industry. This enforced break-up of families is a continuing source of misery and frustration.

The calculated provision of inferior education for blacks, central to the apartheid design, has long been a cause of student complaint. It has for many years been the source of militant and increasingly angry student protest.

Clearly, no group – let alone a majority of the population – could be expected to acquiesce in such treatment. Even as the Government launched its apartheid programme, it took powers to deal with the inevitable challenge from blacks. The Suppression of Communism Act 1950 was passed, an Act which defined 'communism' as seeking any form of social, political, industrial or economic change by 'unlawful acts or omissions, or by means which include the promotion of disturbance or disorder'. Liberalism was equated with communism, and, when in 1952 a peaceful campaign of passive resistance against unjust laws was launched, twenty of its leaders in the Transvaal were convicted under the Act, despite (with a few avowed exceptions) their never having been communists in any accepted meaning of the word.

During the late 1950s, black opposition to restrictive laws became increasingly vociferous. As opposition grew, the ANC in 1955 helped organize a mass 'Congress of the People' at which the Freedom Charter (Annex 5) was adopted. The Congress was broken up, and 156 black leaders were charged with treason (a word, like 'communism', which in the South African legal lexicon is so far removed from its ordinary meaning as to be unrecognizable). The trial dragged on for years, and both the ANC and the (rival) PAC planned nationwide peaceful demonstrations against the 'pass' laws for March 1960. The leaders of both organizations urged non-violence, but inevitably, as crowds assembled throughout the country, there were outbursts of emotion. In most cases the crowds were dispersed by the police without incident, but in others the police lost control. At Sharpeville, on 21 March 1960, sixty-nine blacks were shot dead.

In keeping with their non-violent stand, both the ANC and PAC called for a Day of Mourning on 28 March 1960, and many thousands of blacks stayed away from work. That same day the Government introduced legislation to ban the ANC and the PAC.

Two days later a state of emergency was declared throughout the country. This gave wide powers to prohibit gatherings, to search people and premises and to resort to force. New powers of detention without trial were introduced; it became an offence to make any statement likely to subvert the Government's authority or to incite others to resist; newspapers could be banned. When the state of emergency was lifted, many of the new powers became permanent features of the country's laws.

By the time the last of the 156 defendants in the treason trial had been acquitted – the prosecutors having failed to establish that the Freedom Charter was a 'communist' document – the outlets for peaceful, passive, non-violent resistance had all been closed. By 1960 it was plain that the apartheid state was determined to put down by violent means peaceful protest of any kind and to clamp down on any organization which sought to mobilize black opinion. It is against this background of total repression, in which all avenues for legitimate protest and non-violent opposition were denied, that the decision of the ANC and the PAC finally to turn to armed resistance must be viewed. At a time when blacks in the United States were able to achieve equality through asserting rights already guaranteed to them in their Constitution, blacks in South Africa were being systematically denuded of any such rights and the opportunity to seek them.

The lifting of the 1960 state of emergency in particular did not end the increased scope of detention without trial. The security laws were extended and are now consolidated in the Internal Security Act 1982. This, among other formidable powers, allows for indefinite preventive detention and the greatly feared s.29 form of indefinite detention 'for interrogation', a power much abused by the security forces. The same Act now contains the power for a Minister to 'ban' organizations and individuals. A banned individual can be required to stay in a certain place, prohibited from attending gatherings and prevented from being quoted. (A copy of one such order, served on Mrs Winnie Mandela, appears as Annex 5.)

Such an array of state powers, many of which are expressly not subject to review by the Courts, coupled with extraordinarily wide definitions of 'communism', 'terrorism', 'treason' and 'sedition', render the country, in the experience of blacks, a police state with a permanent state of emergency – so much so

Fearful of its electrification, Soweto (Johannesburg) students have destroyed their school fence. (Photo: Jeremy Pope)

After the firebomb. The headquarters of the Release Mandela Campaign, Johannesburg. (Photo: Jeremy Pope)

that lawyers with whom we spoke had been surprised that the Government had found it necessary to impose a formal state of emergency in 1985 unless it were to placate its right wing.

This move, however, saw three developments. First, power to make mass arrests and detention without trial was extended to every single member of the police force, the railways police, the prison service and the army. Second, the final vestiges of legal control over the authorities were removed by preventing the courts from setting aside orders made under the emergency regulations, and in advance all state officials were made immune from liability both civil and criminal for all unlawful acts (except those in which a complainant could prove bad faith). Third, press censorship was provided for, with bans on photographs and access to affected areas.

Without question, these increased powers contributed significantly to the level of state violence used during the state of emergency.

Violence during the Group's Visit

We came to a country in turmoil, but one in which whites were, in the main, insulated from what was going on around them. As one newspaper editor commented, listeners to the BBC World Service knew more of events in South Africa than did the whites living there. Treated to bland reports from the Government-controlled television and radio services, whites had to look to the English-language press to discover something of what was taking place. This, too, is far from free. It labours under immense difficulties, prevented from reporting much of what is taking place and prohibited from quoting 'banned' persons.

Not only this, but newspapers are severely hindered in their endeavours to cover the unrest. By law they must take 'reasonable steps' to verify the accuracy of their reports. This has been interpreted very strictly and the onus of proof is on the newspaper. The *Cape Times*, for example, is being prosecuted for its coverage of the killing by police of alleged ANC guerrillas at Guguletu. All of the dead were shot in the head and eye-witnesses reportedly claimed that in some cases this had happened after the victims had been disabled. We were told that a large number of prosecutions against journalists were pending. Nor are pressures only legal. The editor of *Die Vaderland*, an Afrikaner newspaper, was recently dismissed after refusing to reduce his coverage of disturbances, and we heard of one other Afrikaner editor who had been under personal and official pressure.

Even as we arrived in February, the level of violence touched new heights when, in Alexandra, police shot and killed a large number of blacks. Day after day the toll grew, with the township sealed off and the blacks meeting live ammunition with stones and home-made petrol bombs. Finally the official death toll reached twenty-four. But when we were subsequently able to visit Alexandra (having been stopped and taken to the police station by the security forces on our first attempt), we heard disquieting stories that suggested a substantially higher death rate: stories of police removing bodies and not returning them for burial, of families forced to bury their dead in secret and of bodies being distributed over a number of hospitals and police morgues.

We were unable to investigate these allegations. We had no power to call the authorities to account. However, we were deeply moved by the account given us by one local resident. Fearing his son might be dead, he had gone to look for him in a hospital morgue. The first body he saw was that of his son, shot several times. Steeling himself from his personal grief, he determined to see how many other bodies there were there and so pretended not to recognize his son. In all, he told us, he counted in excess of forty bodies, all of them victims of gunshot wounds, in one morgue alone.

Throughout our first visit to Alexandra we were shadowed by Casspirs (armoured personnel carriers), despite our protests to the security forces and our anxiety not to be seen as being 'escorted' or afforded protection by the Government. Their oppressive presence was to become familiar to us. Frequently we encountered them, ready to seal off roads leading in and out of townships and to stop anyone, such as ourselves, who

In the shadow of the Casspirs. Lord Barber and Swaran Singh. (Photo: Moni Malhoutra)

appeared out of place. On occasion, some of our Group were able to blend with residents and walk past the Casspirs into areas experiencing particular tension.

Clearly the police were confronted with an enormously difficult task in having to try to maintain law and order in an atmosphere seething with discontent, distrust and hostility. But equally clearly they chose in the main to adopt an aggressive and ruthless approach. As evidence to the 1985 Kannemeyer Commission makes plain, the police do not hesitate to fire lethal buckshot into crowds of unarmed black civilians, even when they are not threatening and are on their way to a funeral. When confronted with an illegal gathering (and two people are sufficient in law to comprise a 'gathering'), the police respond with a degree of force wholly out of line with that either required by the circumstances or permitted by law.

Everywhere we went we received complaints about police and army conduct. So widespread and so consistent were these complaints of excessive force, of gratuitous beatings, of point-blank shootings, that to us they had an unmistakable ring of truth.

There was a similarly widespread and consistent pattern of complaints about the treatment of detainees. We spoke to numerous people of all races who recounted to us how, while in detention, they had been assaulted and even tortured – in some cases being brought close to drowning by having their heads held down in buckets of water dowsed with tear-gas.

Nor are we alone in accepting the general veracity of these complaints; despite their generally restricted jurisdiction, courts have on more than one occasion in recent weeks been able to make orders restraining the security forces from illegal acts of violence. Indeed, it would be surprising if, given the freedom from accountability granted to the security forces, abuses did not occur.

The Minister of Law and Order maintained in discussions with us that the police invariably act responsibly, with restraint and within the law. The evidence, however, suggests otherwise.

One difficulty confronting the police is simply the breadth of the prohibitions against blacks. There has been a general ban on open-air meetings (with special permission being granted only rarely) for over ten years. This means that even a funeral can amount to a technical breach of the law. Such a breach is no doubt magnified by the inevitability – given both that the deceased are frequently victims of police action and the absence of any other avenue of political expression – that a funeral itself will take on the form of a political rally to accord martyrdom to the dead.

These are times when passions run high, and feeling against the security forces is close to flash point. When the police presence is oppressive, all too often violence flares and one funeral leads to others. But, we observed, when the police adopted a low profile almost invariably funerals, even mass funerals, passed off peacefully.

Not only are funerals highly emotional events, but they also follow deeply etched cultural patterns. The typical black funeral commences with an all-night vigil at the home of the deceased, and, after a service and the burial, it concludes with a ceremonial washing of the hands. We learnt of unprovoked attacks by security forces lobbing tear-gas into houses during vigils, sjamboking* women and children and deliberately wrecking the barrels of water awaiting the return of mourners from the graveside. No doubt on occasion the security forces believed some offence was being committed, but the suddenness and savagery of their reaction are indefensible.

One Minister in particular argued strenuously that police presence at funerals was essential to maintain law and order and listed a number of funerals where police had stayed away and some trouble had ensured. He did not, however, point to any instance where anything approaching the violence of which we had learned had occurred when police were not in evidence.

Claims that the security forces provoke violence are confirmed by our own experience. On our very first visit to a township, Johannesburg's Soweto, we were confronted by the spectacle of a policeman chasing and shooting at an apparently unarmed person, and this not 15 yards away from us. Almost whenever we encountered armoured personnel carriers, their occupants and their weapons gave the unmistakable impression of menace. On one occasion, one of our Co-Chairmen was almost pushed in the stomach with the barrel of a gun by a white lance-corporal while his superior looked on.

In general, the Government gave us unimpeded access to people and places; we went to some where its writ did not run. However, on occasion it appeared that its orders were not obeyed by its own intelligence agents. In our travels through the Karoo, in the heart of the country, they flaunted their prior knowledge of aspects of our travel programme (although we had not communicated this to any officials). They parked conspicuously in hedges near where our light plane was to land, followed our cars and generally advertised their presence even in an area where four United Democratic Front (UDF) officials from Cradock had been murdered only months before, in circumstances widely believed to suggest their involvement. In Port Elizabeth intelligence agents staked out the hotel where we were to meet with UDF officials whom they were keen to detain.

* A sjambok is a whip of hardened rubber with a heavy tip.

The meeting had to be cancelled. People who had journeyed from Prieska to meet us in De Aar were detained on their way home. We protested immediately to the Department of Foreign Affairs and were subsequently informed that they would be released after questioning. A minor driving offence was said to be the cause.

As we moved about the country we became persuaded that there was, in fact, a systematic and seemingly orchestrated campaign of intimidation directed at activities in the democratic cause. In Atteridgeville, near Pretoria, we arrived to find that one house had been the subject of a grenade attack the night before, and a second firebombed. In Johannesburg's Braamfontein business area too, the offices of the Release Mandela Campaign were firebombed. In Moutse, we learnt of violence used to intimidate residents whose only request was for a plebiscite on their future.

When persons with gunshot wounds seek medical help, the police are advised and charges of 'public violence' follow, based on the doubtful premise that if a person was the victim of gunfire he must have been taking part in illegal activity. This causes many children, in particular, not to seek medical assistance when wounded. Instead, they operate on each other, to cut out buckshot and bullets as best they can, hoping that the inevitable complications will not be unduly severe.

In early May, police broke into Arcadia High School in Bronteheuwel after coloured pupils had been involved in a demonstration, and whipped their victims with sjamboks. The School Committee reported that the police seemed to take 'particular pleasure to damage the faces of the pupils' and that 'children had to drag themselves between two rows of policemen as the sjambok blows rained down on them'. Five were hospitalized; a number were scarred for life; and one reportedly faced the likelihood of losing an eye. In all, two pupils were charged with 'public violence' but released two days later without any allegations against them. Indeed, we heard, with depressing repetition, accounts of violence directed by the security forces against children, of children brutally whipped, of schoolrooms teargassed and of difficulties experienced by parents in locating children taken by the police.

One such instance we were able to witness for ourselves, for on a journey into the Northern Transvaal we were accompanied by a local lawyer, who was asked by a mother to locate her child. He had reportedly disappeared after a bus in which he had been travelling to a funeral with a youth group had been stopped and its occupants fired on by police. After encountering denials at one police station, we tracked the boy, of about 14 years, to the Groblersdal police station. Although the duty officer was helpful initially, it took the lawyer over two hours of persistent effort to overcome the reluctance of successive police and security men to produce him. Threatened with a complaint to his Minister, the senior officer finally produced the boy. He was limping; his face was bruised; and his shirt was splattered in blood. He said he had not been fed or given medical attention: his injuries had been received while he was being arrested, but he had also been slapped at the police station. He was denied bail on a charge of 'trespass' (he had been found taking refuge on a white-owned farm). We could not imagine that the boy's mother would have had any chance of overcoming the police's obduracy when it took an experienced and skilful white laywer so long to do so.

While we were in South Africa, we encountered or heard of violence and its manifestations nearly everywhere we went. We did not have to seek it out: it was a daily phenomenon.

In particular, we could not escape the huge pall of smoke that hung over Crossroads for much of our second visit. There, we were informed, black vigilantes, with active backing from the security forces, were attacking supporters of the UDF, including women and children, and setting fire to their shanties. Some thirty-three were killed, many more injured and upwards of 30,000 rendered homeless.

From what we heard and saw, there appeared to be a pattern of vigilante violence directed against blacks agitating for change in the *status quo* by some of those who have a stake of sorts in 'the system' and are being encouraged by the authorities to preserve it in this way.

In the townships these elements tend to comprise town

councillors (some of whom profit in an urban setting rife with corruption) and the 'leaders' in squatter camps, some of whom impose rents in the form of protection money on those with no option but to squat. These elements feel threatened by the democratic movement. Their fears, whether physical or financial, lend themselves readily to exploitation, although we recognize, of course, that many of those within 'the system' do not seek to defend it and actively support the democratic movement. However, there is a substantial body of evidence, including that gathered by Black Sash and other human rights organizations, that official agencies, in a wish to promote 'black-on-black' violence and the notion that blacks are divided among themselves, give some degree of encouragement to vigilante groups.

In a situation such as that in South Africa, blacks who 'collaborate' with the Government obviously make themselves vulnerable. It is a fact of life that in any uprising against the oppression of an army of occupation – which the South African security forces are seen as being – those who collaborate with the occupiers are among the first victims. For a European equivalent, one need look no further than the French Resistance, whose members perpetrated premeditated violence on those of their people who were seen as siding with the occupying power.

Mirroring the growth of black vigilantism is the ominous development of white vigilantes. There are indications that some whites are fuelling, and participating in, black vigilante activity, and this must be a cause for serious concern in the future. As matters stood while we were in the country, the occasional group of youthful white racists would perpetrate aimless and gratuitous violence on blacks.

After the State of Emergency

The state of emergency was lifted while we were in the country, on 7 March 1986, to no noticeable effect. Levels of unrest had escalated, not subsided, throughout the period the state of emergency was in force and continued to escalate after it was lifted.

Statistics in South Africa are far from reliable. Some include 'homeland' areas; others do not; and some seem slanted to suit government perspectives. None the less, since the present unrest began over 1,700 people have been killed, as well as twenty while in police custody. Most of the latter were under the age of 25; one was only 13. During the state of emergency alone, the security forces admit to having killed about half of the 792 whose deaths were recorded in official figures. Many of these were under the age of 18. During the state of emergency too an estimated 11,500 were detained without charge, among them well over 2,000 children under the age of 16. An additional 25,000 people, many of them young, were arrested on charges of 'public violence'. Only a very small proportion of these were ever convicted, as most of the charges were dropped. By way of example, one 11-year-old child, arrested for 'public violence', was kept in custody for fifty-seven days before being released. Applications for bail were refused, but finally the charge was dropped. At present about 150 people are being killed each month.

With the lifting of the emergency, a number of detainees were released; others were transferred to be held without charge under different legislation. Most of the political leaders detained during the emergency were not released, but held awaiting trial.

Shortly after the ending of the emergency, a Supreme Court decision held that the wording of a number of banning orders was defective in that it did not comply with the technical requirements of the Internal Security Act; the court could not have inquired into the substance of the orders. Several activists – including Mrs Winnie Mandela – were immediate beneficiaries of the decision, but their fate in the longer term awaits ministerial decision.

Yet the ending of the state of emergency in no way signalled an end to the violence and the counter-violence. If it had been imposed to bring the situation under control, it had palpably failed. Events had increasingly passed out of the Government's control, and the toll of life and property continues.

When announcing the lifting of the state of emergency, the Government foreshadowed increased powers for the security forces. These are now before Parliament. If enacted, such are their scope that South Africa will unquestionably pass even further into a permanent state of emergency. On top of his already formidable powers under the Internal Security Act, the Minister of Law and Order will be able to declare 'unrest areas' (a euphemism for a state of emergency limited in area) where total control over the area and its inhabitants will pass to the security forces. In an additional measure, police are to be given the power of detention without trial of up to 180 days, in addition to their other powers to detain.

The Nassau Accord called upon the South African Government to 'terminate the existing state of emergency'. From a technical viewpoint, this has come to pass; in reality, however, South Africa is sliding even further into a permanent state of emergency in terms of the ordinary laws of the land.

Chapter 3
The Release of Nelson Mandela and Others

From the beginning, we recognized the essential significance in any political settlement of one man – Nelson Mandela. Imprisoned these last twenty-four years, latterly in Pollsmoor Prison, he is an isolated and lonely figure, bearing his incarceration with courage and fortitude, anxious to be reunited with his wife and family but determined that this can only be in circumstances which allow for his unconditional release, along with colleagues and fellow political prisoners, and permit them all to take part in normal political activity.

A symbol to many, Nelson Mandela can be said to represent all those imprisoned, detained, banned or in exile for their opposition to apartheid: men like Wilton Mcquai, Govan Mbeki, Zephania Mothupeng and John Ganya on Robben Island; Walter Sisulu, Ahmed Kathrada, Raymond Mhlaba, Andrew Mlangeni and Oscar Mpetha, also in Pollsmoor; Elias Matsoaledi and Harry Gwala in Johannesburg; Patrick Lekota and Popo Molefe in Modderbee; and many others. Certainly, that was the hope expressed by him in the statement, conveyed by his daughter, Miss Zindzi Mandela, to a meeting at the Jabulani Amphitheatre on 10 February 1985. The general question of political trials and the release of detainees is one we will return to later in our Report.

Mr Mandela is himself a political prisoner. In 1964, he and nine others were convicted on a charge of sabotage. In his statement from the dock at the Rivonia Trial, he set out the reasons which led him to do what he did – the lengths to which the ANC had gone to avoid violence since its inception in 1912 and the repressive policies upholding apartheid which, he argued, had finally forced upon them a reactive violence.

He told the court that when the ANC had been declared an unlawful organization, it had refused to dissolve and had gone underground. It was only after that, in June 1961, that he had come to the conclusion that violence was inevitable and that it would be unrealistic and wrong for African leaders to continue with a policy of non-violence when the Government had 'met our demands with violence'. Thereafter, it was decided that the ANC would 'no longer disapprove of properly controlled sabotage', by which means the economy would be damaged and international attention attracted. He remains deprived of his liberty because he is not prepared to disavow that decision. As he himself has put it: 'I am in prison as the representative of the people and the African National Congress, which was banned. What freedom am I being offered while the organization of the people remains banned?' (Statement, 10 February 1985)

But Nelson Mandela is also a symbol for blacks not only of their lack of political freedom but also of their struggle to attain it. He is a potent inspiration for much of the political activity of black South Africans. His role in the management of the Defiance Campaign of 1952 and his leadership of Umkhonto we Sizwe (Spear of the Nation), for which he remains imprisoned, together with the manner in which he has borne his fate, have established him as a legend in his own lifetime. His suffering is seen as the suffering of all who are the victims of apartheid. The campaign for his release has been the galvanizing spur for rising black political consciousness across South Africa. His name is emblazoned across the length and breadth of black South Africa.

In particular, the call for his freedom has developed into the centrepiece of the demand for a political settlement. It is the shorthand for the proposition that, as his daughter Zindzi conveyed it, 'There is an alternative to the inevitable bloodbath.'

But we also recognize that, for some whites, he represents something rather different. Their fears, if unfounded, are real none the less. They include the belief that Nelson Mandela is a man of violence and that violence could not be contained on his release; the fear that, as one of the principal black nationalists, his sole aim is to achieve a hand-over of state power from white to black; and the fear that his release would be the signal for chaos and destruction. Most of these fears have been fuelled by the Government's own campaign against Mr Mandela and the ANC. To that extent, they are self-induced, but they are real for all that and cannot be ignored.

Nelson Mandela has indeed become a living legend. Just as the gaoling of nationalist leaders like Mahatma Gandhi and Jomo Kenyatta invested them with a unique aura and helped galvanize resistance to the colonial power, so, we believe, the imprisonment of Nelson Mandela is a self-defeating course for the South African Government to take.

With each month and year of further incarceration, the difficulties of the Government will grow. While fit at present, he is a man of 67. It would be wise to heed the words of Soren Kierkegaard: 'The tyrant dies and his rule ends: the martyr dies and his rule begins.'

Discussions with Nelson Mandela were obviously going to be essential to our work. Initially, arranging such discussions did not prove easy. Other visiting groups had been denied access, and the South African authorities approached our request with great caution. We also asked to see other political prisoners and detainees in Pollsmoor and on Robben Island.

During the preliminary visit, General Obasanjo was permitted to see Mr Mandela. Thereafter the full Group met with him on two occasions, although not with other detainees. In all these meetings we were conscious of our responsibility to Nelson Mandela himself. As recently as 10 February 1985, when referring to suggestions for his conditional release, he had referred to the constraints that custody imposes. 'Only free men can negotiate,' he said. 'Prisoners cannot enter into contracts.' It was essential, we felt, that we should meet and talk with him. We were equally determined that those conversations should neither compromise nor embarrass him. We reiterate that intent in drawing on those conversations for the purposes of our Report.

The Group approached the meetings with Mr Mandela with another measure of care. It was impossible not to be aware of the mythology surrounding him, but, equally, we were determined that it should not colour our impressions or influence our judgment. As far as possible, we resolved to approach these meetings with an open mind.

We were first struck by his physical authority – by his immaculate appearance, his apparent good health and his commanding presence. In his manner he exuded authority and received the respect of all around him, including his gaolers. That in part seemed to reflect his own philosophy of separating people from policy.

His authority clearly extends throughout the nationalist movement, although he constantly reiterated that he could not speak for his colleagues in the ANC, that, apart from his personal viewpoint, any concerted view must come after proper consultation with all concerned and that his views could carry weight only when expressed collectively through the ANC.

There was no visible distance of outlook, however, between Nelson Mandela and the ANC leadership in Lusaka. He was at pains to point out that his own authority derived solely from his position within the organization, and in so far as he was able to reflect the popular will.

Second, we found his attitude to others outside the ANC reasonable and conciliatory. He did not conceal his differences with Chief Buthelezi, and he was conscious of the divisions which had arisen among the black community. Nevertheless, he was confident that, if he were to be released from prison, the unity of all black leaders, including Chief Buthelezi, could be achieved. The ANC, as the vanguard of the liberation movement, had particular responsibilities, but the fact that freedom fighters belonged to a variety of organizations was both a challenge to, and an indictment of, the ANC. He stressed repeatedly the importance of the unity of the whole nationalist movement.

In our discussions Nelson Mandela also took care to emphasize his desire for reconciliation across the divide of colour. He described himself as a deeply committed South African nation-

alist but added that South African nationalists came in
than one colour – there were white people, coloured peopl[
Indian people who were also deeply committed South Afri[
nationalists. He pledged himself anew to work for a multiracia[
society in which all would have a secure place.

He recognized the fears of many white people, which had
been intensified by the Government's own propaganda, but
emphasized the importance of minority groups being given a
real sense of security in any new society in South Africa.

That desire for good will was palpable. The Minister of
Justice, together with two senior officials, was present at the
start of our second meeting and Mr Mandela pressed him to
remain, saying he had nothing to hide and no objection to the
Minister hearing the discussion. It was his strongly stated view
that if the circumstances could be created in which the
Government and the ANC could talk, some of the problems
which arose solely through lack of contact could be eliminated.
The fact of talking was essential in the building of mutual confidence.

Third, we were impressed by the consistency of his beliefs.
He emphasized that he was a nationalist, not a communist, and
that his principles were unchanged from those to which he
subscribed when the Freedom Charter was drawn up in 1955.
Those principles included the necessity for the unity and political emancipation of all Africans in the land of their birth; the
need for a multiracial society, free from any kind of racial,
religious or political discrimination; the paramountcy of democratic principles and of political and human rights; and equality
of opportunity. He held to the view that the Freedom Charter
embodied policies which amounted to a devastating attack on
discrimination in all its ramifications – economic, social and
political.

While it called for a new order, this was not to be on the basis
of any change in the system of production apart from certain
key sectors. He argued that he and his colleagues had been to
court because of the Freedom Charter, that the court had deliber-
ated for four years before giving its verdict that the Crown had
failed to establish its case, and the Freedom Charter was not a

document designed to establish even socialism in South Africa. He recognized it was a document which some might not consider 'progressive' enough; it was none the less one to which he still subscribed and which, he believed, could have a wide appeal to whites as well as to blacks.

Our fourth impression was that Nelson Mandela was a man who had been driven to armed struggle only with the greatest reluctance, solely in the absence of any other alternative to the violence of the apartheid system, and never as an end in itself. It was a course of action which he argued had been forced upon him, as he explained at his trial in 1964: 'A time comes in the life of any nation when there remains only two choices – submit or fight. That time has now come to South Africa. We shall not submit and we have no choice but to hit back by all the means in our power in defence or our people, our future and our freedom.'

At that trial he had gone to great lengths to show that Umkhonto we Sizwe's policy was to avoid hurting civilians and instead to concentrate on damaging property. That policy was apparently maintained up until 1983, when the ANC's first car bomb exploded at Air Force Headquarters in Pretoria. Yet Mr Mandela even then had expressed his sadness over the incident and had said from prison: 'It was a tragic accident . . . we aim for buildings and property. It might be that someone gets killed in the fire, in the heat of battle, but we do not believe in assassination.'

We questioned Nelson Mandela extensively about his views on violence. The ANC, he said, had for many years operated as a non-violent organization and had been forced into armed struggle only because it became the unavoidable response to the violence of apartheid. He stressed that violence could never be an ultimate solution and that the nature of human relationships required negotiation. He was not in a position to renounce the use of violence as a condition of his release, and we recognized that in the circumstances currently prevailing in South Africa it would be unreasonable to expect that of him or anyone else.

Fifth, there was no doubting Nelson Mandela's welcome for the Commonwealth initiative and his personal desire to help.

With Winnie Mandela – Ted Scott, Swaran Singh, Nita Barrow, Malcolm Fraser, WM, John Malecela, Lord Barber, General Obasanjo. (Photo: Moni Malhoutra)

While emphasizing that he could not speak for the ANC, he expressed his personal acceptance of the Group's negotiating concept★ as a starting point. He made it clear that his personal acceptance stood, regardless of whether or not it was acceptable to the South African Government, but he wanted his views to be those of the movement and not simply his own, and there would be need for consultation with his fellow prisoners (both in Pollsmoor and on Robben Island) and with the ANC in Lusaka.

He believed that if a positive response by the ANC and the Government were to be synchronized – the Government withdrawing the army and the police from the townships and taking other agreed steps, while the ANC agreed, at the same time, to a suspension of violence and to negotiations – there should be no difficulty with implementation. He acknowledged, however, that his release would not be enough to lessen violence.

★ The concept is discussed in Chapter 6.

He and his colleagues would have to take on the active role of persuading people to call off violent activities and to respect the negotiating process. This meant that the negotiating process had to be fully credible and kept so by the Government.

Our sixth, and final, impression was of a man who yearned for his freedom and who longed to be reunited with his family, but who would never accept it under what he called 'humiliating conditions'. As he put it in his statement of 10 February 1985:

I cherish my own freedom dearly, but I care even more for your freedom. Too many have died since I went to prison. Too many have suffered for the love of freedom. I owe it to their widows, to their orphans, to their mothers and their fathers who have grieved and wept for them.

Not only have I suffered during these long lonely wasted years. I am no less life-loving than you are. But I cannot sell the birthright of the people to be free.

Only free men can negotiate. Prisoners cannot enter into contracts. Your freedom and mine cannot be separated.

We accept that the release of Nelson Mandela presents the South African Government with a difficult dilemma. Having held him too long in prison, there is a growing realization in Government circles that any benefits of incarceration are outweighed by the disadvantages which daily become more apparent. Yet to release him now, as some in Government say is their wish, would be to do so into conditions much changed from ten, or even five, years ago. In a mood of unrest and upheaval, with growing black awareness and political protest being matched by increasing anxiety among whites and the rise of white extremism, the Government has expressed the fear that his release might result in an uncontrollable explosion of violence.

We do not hold this view. Provided the negotiating process were agreed, Mr Mandela's own voice would appeal for calm. We believe his authority would secure it.

In our discussions with the ANC, it has become clear that they, along with every black group within South Africa, see the unconditional release of Nelson Mandela and other political prisoners and detainees as a necessary and crucial step towards a settlement. Negotiations cannot take place in the absence of the people's authentic leaders. The release into South African society of those leaders would lead logically to negotiations, through a process of normal political activity, on behalf of legally recognized organizations. No other equation is possible. No piecemeal or more limited approach can possibly succeed.

Without this first step, linked to a wider package, the ANC and others will have no basis for believing in the state violence of the apartheid system ever abating and will not be persuaded to suspend violence themselves. The struggle and the killing will continue with greater intensity. The cycle of violence will remain unbroken.

Mr Mandela, according to all the evidence, is a unifying, commanding and popular leader. Recent opinion polls, as well as our personal observations, revealed that blacks, Indians and coloureds look overwhelmingly to Nelson Mandela as the leader of a non-racial South Africa.

To disregard Nelson Mandela, by continuing his imprisonment, would be to discard an essential and heroic figure in any political settlement in South Africa. His freedom is a key component in any hope of a peaceful resolution of a conflict which otherwise will prove all-consuming.

Our judgment of Nelson Mandela has been formed as the result of lengthy discussions with him, spanning three meetings. He impressed us as an outstandingly able and sincere person whose qualities of leadership were self-evident. We found him unmarked by any trace of bitterness despite his long imprisonment. His overriding concern was for the welfare of all races in South Africa in a just society; he longed to be allowed to contribute to the process of reconciliation. We all agreed that it was tragic that a man of his outstanding capabilities should continue to be denied the opportunity to help shape his country's future, especially as that is so clearly his own profound wish.

That he is a fervent nationalist cannot be denied; but of his supposed communism, either now or in the past, we found no trace. In that respect we clearly differ from the Government which has resorted to the most dubious of methods to denigrate his reputation.

Central to the Nassau Accord was a call for the immediate and unconditional release of Nelson Mandela, and all other political prisoners. That call remains unheeded. It is one to which we attach the highest importance.

Chapter 4

The Establishment of Political Freedom

It is not for our Group to attempt to prescribe what the future constitutional structures of South Africa ought to be – a point made time and time again in our meetings. The essence of establishing these must lie in creating conditions of political freedom in which the people, *all* the people, through their authentic representatives, can exercise free choice about their future. The legitimacy of what emerges would then rest on the necessary foundation of the consent of the governed.

State President Botha, in addressing the President's Council on 15 May, spelt out certain norms and values which he considered fundamental and which he said would have to be entrenched in any new dispensation. These included, as he put it, the 'realization of the democratic ideal, since it is the Government's accepted principle that only democratic institutions can meet the demands of justice and fairness'. This democratic settlement had to accommodate 'the legitimate political aspirations of all South Africa's communities'. Further, it must therefore be multi-cultural and must protect minority rights. Basic human freedoms – such as freedom of worship and faith, equality of opportunity and the absence of discrimination, the sanctity of law and of individual liberty – must be respected.

While these may be laudable aims, the attention of the black majority is concentrated upon the denial of basic democratic freedoms under the present system. Their credibility as genuine goals will be judged on future developments. Blacks, of course, do not have the vote in white South Africa, and, as explained earlier, the development of apartheid through the Bantustan (or 'homeland') system has had the practical effect of depriving millions of blacks of their South African citizenship, making them 'foreigners' in the land of their birth.

For those who remain 'citizens', basic freedoms are either non-existent, or too severely circumscribed to be meaningful. The legal mechanisms to stifle political activity are many and varied, and some are mentioned elsewhere in our Report. By way of illustration, freedom of assembly, for one, is severely curtailed. As we have already noted, there is a general ban on outdoor meetings without specific permission; indoor meetings are subject to police and magisterial controls through blanket or specific banning orders. There are also limitations on what may be discussed with such topics as rent strikes, economic boycotts and the like forbidden by law.

The banning of most important black political organizations (and thereby meetings to discuss and further the aims of those organizations) represents a major impediment to freedom of association. Similarly, arbitrary powers to detain and to 'ban' individuals are used to harass and immobilize legitimate political organizations. In recent months this has been particularly so in the case of the UDF, which has not only suffered from a sustained attack on its leadership through legal channels, but those whose members and officials have been hounded, harassed and often attacked by vigilantes. The black churches however, have so far been spared the full imposition of these restrictions. They have thus assumed an important role in the struggle for freedom. However, they, too, now feel under threat.

Freedom of speech and expression is also subject to draconian limitations. Newspapers are effectively debarred from covering certain topics and are not permitted to publish news of detained or banned persons. Those who defy the law and publish the views of, for example, Oliver Tambo, risk prosecution and imprisonment – and it is for this that the editor of the *Cape Times*, Anthony Heard, is presently before the court. Apart from ministerial and magesterial controls, newspapers are subject to extra-legal sanctions (such as the threat to withdraw advertising). Extensive powers curtail the ability of journalists to report on areas of unrest and disturbance.

Given such a broad panoply of powers, it is difficult to see

General Obasanjo addresses a crowded congregation in Graff-Reinet (Photo: Hugh Craft)

any residual elements of political freedom surviving. In such circumstances, too, the distinction between political organizations which are banned outright and those still tolerated but subjected to the whim of arbitrary power becomes increasingly academic.

A genuine process of dialogue leading to a sustainable political settlement can take place only in an environment of free political activity. This involves a number of elements.

First, all existing restrictions on the holding of meetings – who may address them, what may be discussed and how they may be reported – must be lifted. Second, all restrictions on the formation and membership of political parties for legitimate political purposes must be removed. Third, all those imprisoned, detained or banned for political reasons must be freed from restriction. Any limits on these freedoms must be consistent with the requirements of a democratic society.

And this, after all, is merely 'normal political activity'. Such political 'normality' has never been known in South Africa. Its establishment requires the creation of an entirely new environment in which dialogue could be pursued with confidence and legitimacy.

The Nassau Accord called on the South African Government to 'establish political freedom and specifically lift the existing ban on the African National Congress and other political parties'.

The Government has made no movement towards this goal. Indeed, recently it has been moving in the opposite direction.

Chapter 5
Prospects for Negotiations

Our first duty was to get an accurate reading of the political pulse of the country. We therefore consulted, as widely as possible, all sectors of South African society. A process of fact-finding was essential if we were to assist the parties in finding the necessary common ground for starting genuine negotiations. What follows is a synopsis of these views as presented to us.

The Position of the South African Government

The attitude of the South African Government was clearly going to be the single most important determining factor. We therefore probed its thinking in depth. We met a large number of Government Ministers, some several times, the Cabinet's Constitutional Committee and the State President himself.

While reaffirming South Africa's position as a sovereign State which could not brook outside interference, Ministers said they had taken careful note of the Nassau Accord's emphasis on negotiation and dialogue in the context of a suspension of violence. It was only on this basis that the Government had been able to persuade the doubters in its own ranks to look seriously at the Accord on the assumption that the Commonwealth was genuine and earnest in its pursuit of a peaceful solution.

There had been much soul-searching in white South Africa, they claimed, in regard to the Commonwealth initiative. Many regarded it as interference in domestic affairs and thought it should not be allowed because South Africa's future was the sole business of the Government; others felt that the presence of the Group would exacerbate an already delicate situation in that it would be seen as supportive of opposition elements hostile to the Government. Additionally, there was a growing impatience with individuals and groups, both internal and external, who were putting forward proposals for change which served only to inject confusion and uncertainty into a prospective negotiating process.

Ministers claimed that a radical movement away from classic apartheid had been under way for at least a decade. Legislation had been introduced repealing or amending some of the more obnoxious and visible apartheid laws (e.g. influx control, mixed marriages), redressing in some measure the social and economic inequalities of the apartheid legal and administrative systems (e.g. housing, education) and amending the Constitution to 'extend democracy' and 'power-sharing' to certain communal groups through the Tricameral Parliament. In the State President's words, apartheid was 'outmoded'.

In this context we noted the assurance conveyed by the Government to us that 'the door was wide open for the first time in South Africa's history, to achievement through negotiations of a political apparatus in South Africa that could satisfy the political aspirations of all the country's communities. Negotiation is the key to the solution of South Africa's problems.'

The position of the South African Government was summarized in a paper handed to the Group by one Minister, which read as follows:

It is the conviction of the Government that any future constitutional dispensation providing for participation by all South African citizens should be the result of negotiations with the leaders of all communities.

The Government will not prescribe who may represent black communities in negotiations on a new constitution for South Africa.

The only condition is that those who participate in the discussions and negotiations should forswear violence as a means of achieving political objectives.

The agenda for political reform is open. In the process of negotiation the Government will not prescribe and will not demand. Give and take will be the guiding principle.

On the part of Government, negotiations will be based on the following premises:

- the principle of a united South Africa, one citizenship and a universal franchise within democratic structures;
- political participation of all communities at all levels on matters of national concern;
- co-responsibility and power-sharing between these communities on matters of national concern;
- the devolution of power as far as possible;
- the protection of minority rights, without one group dominating the other;
- the sovereignty of the law as the basis for the protection of the fundamental rights of individuals as well as groups;
- equality before the law, and
- the protection of human dignity, life, liberty and property of all, regardless of colour, race, creed or religion.

The South African Government also confirms that the situation of detainees or prisoners will be reviewed as violence recedes and normality returns; and

- it is positively committed to and actively involved in contributing to the peace, stability and development of the Southern African region.

In the course of our conversations with various Ministers, some of these ideas were elaborated. We were assured that all the necessary decisions regarding the central question of power-sharing had already been taken. The key question was not whether there was going to be power-sharing, but in what manner. Future change would have to be perceived within the context of the Government's reform programme as articulated. Our Group might have a role in furthering negotiations in peaceful conditions by establishing common ground between the parties.

A fuller statement containing a summary of the State President's announcements on constitutional development was also handed to us by another Minister, which is reproduced at Annex 6.

The South African Government's position defies succinct summary. It has perfected a specialized political vocabulary which, while saying one thing, means quite another. Thus the stated approach to negotiations was qualified by a number of provisos, which were repeatedly underlined during the course of our discussions. While apartheid was declared 'outmoded', 'finished' and, indeed, 'dead', the Government's objective was the exercise of political rights and freedoms within the structures of 'groups' or 'communities'. South Africa was 'a nation of minorities' and future constitutional arrangements would give expression to individual aspirations only within the confines of their ethnic groups. Group rights were to take precedence over individual rights, with built-in assurances of no one group being dominated by others. Western democratic practice had no relevance to South African conditions.

Similar qualifications emerged in respect of the objectives of the Government's programme of reform and the basic parameters of any negotiation. The Government's proclaimed commitment to a 'united South Africa' excluded the four 'independent homelands' and reaffirmed the goal of independence for the remaining 'self-governing' ones. 'Common citizenship for all South Africans' similarly excluded all black South Africans resident in the 'independent homelands', including the millions forcibly removed there. 'Universal franchise' would be exercised 'within structures chosen by South Africans jointly', namely within the group context that rules out the possibility of a common electoral roll. Full political participation by means of power-sharing, and co-operation on matters deemed to be of 'national concern', would be subject to 'self-determination' for each group in respect of its 'own affairs', an expression with very wide meaning in the South African constitutional context.

Despite the objectives mentioned in the above two paragraphs, we were assured that the agenda at a negotiation would be open, and our discussions with the Government proceeded on that assumption.

We were struck immediately by the Government's attitude to the question of violence. The Government was deeply concerned that its reform programme had elicited no response from the black community and that violence was on the increase. There was no recognition that apartheid itself was sustained through violence and that the inequities and injustices it perpetrated fostered violence. Nor was there any

Lord Barber with ANC President Oliver Tambo in Lusaka, Zambia. (Photo: Hugh Craft)

Malcolm Fraser with Dr Allan Boesak, Patron of the UDF, at Port Elizabeth. (Photo: Jeremy Pope)

Malcolm Fraser, Emeka Anyaoku (Commonwealth Deputy Secretary-General), Bishop Desmond Tutu, General Obasanjo and Moni Malhoutra (Commonwealth Secretariat). (Photo: Hugh Craft)

Lord Barber, Winnie Mandela, Ismael Ayob (Attorney for Nelson Mandela) and General Obasanjo at Sandton, Johannesburg. (Photo: Malcolm Fraser)

willingness to admit the militarization of the townships and the well-documented brutality of some elements of the security forces were themselves provoking a violent response.

So far as the Government was concerned, the overwhelming responsibility for violence lay upon the ANC and its supporters. The uprisings in the townships, the failure of blacks to come forward to co-operate with the Government, the commercial and school boycotts testified, in the view of the Government, to the dominance of the ANC by 'communist-controlled terrorists' committed to the violent overthrow of the legitimate government.

The Position of Other Parties and Organizations

THE AFRICAN NATIONAL CONGRESS (ANC)

In assessing the position of the ANC and its leadership several factors need to be taken into account, namely that the ANC is a banned organization in South Africa; that Nelson Mandela and many others of its leadership have been imprisoned for almost a quarter of a century; that the ANC and its objectives enjoy considerable popular support among black South Africans; and that the role of its external leadership and the nature of the ANC struggle are central to the South African political problem.

The Government acknowledged that we would need to consult with the ANC leadership both within and outside South Africa. It facilitated our meetings with Nelson Mandela in Pollsmoor Prison on three occasions.

Close contacts were established at an early stage with the ANC's external leadership which led to two formal consultations with ANC President Oliver Tambo, and members of the ANC Executive in Lusaka.

The ANC leadership told us that their immediate reaction to the setting up of the Group had been one of disappointment. Their hopes had been raised by the debate in Nassau and the prospect of increased international pressure on the Government through sanctions against Pretoria. Instead, the Group had been established and, in their view, it would assist in relieving the pressures on the South African Government which had been building up in the period before Nassau. We were nevertheless warmly welcomed as the ANC had a keen interest in hearing what the Group felt it might be able to do.

In the ANC's view, a peaceful resolution of the crisis in South Africa would become possible if the Government took immediately the steps elaborated in the Nassau Accord. These coincided with what the people of South Africa had been demanding for many years – but to date it appeared that the Botha regime was interested not in negotiations but only in pursuing a war against the people. Dialogue of a kind had also been going on for many years – but statements and counter-statements were not enough. Negotiations went beyond dialogue and should address the essential issue, the elimination of apartheid.

In the ANC analysis, the Government was projecting itself as embarking on a process of reform because of the pressures it was under. These sprang from various sources: the continuing threat of further sanctions and the growing sense of isolation from the international community was one; the escalating conflict and violence, which had developed a momentum of its own, was another. Both would be crucial determinants of change. Immense pressure would be required before the South African Government would be ready to negotiate seriously. At the moment, the Government purported to be promoting dialogue by establishing a National Statutory Council as an alternative to the fourth Chamber of Parliament, but it would be a consultative body without power. Along with the Tri-cameral Parliament it had been rejected by the people because it was not what they were demanding – liberation from racist oppression, full political power and full political rights.

The ANC expressed great interest in the South African Government's response to our mandate because only then would it be able to make its own contribution. If the Government was prepared to shift its ground and indicate its readiness for fundamental change this would impact on the

ANC view. Their assessment was, however, that nothing had changed and nothing would change. If that proved to be the case, then the conditions for negotiation did not exist.

The ANC placed much emphasis on the release of Nelson Mandela, a crucial step which recognized that it was not possible for negotiation to take place in the absence of the people's authentic leaders. A prerequisite for talking to the Government was that it should be through the people's recognized leaders, not through the ones the Government chose to identify. Without this essential first step the conflict would continue.

On the question of violence, the ANC expressed concern that the situation as it had developed over the years was one of conflict and violence escalating and developing a momentum of its own. This likelihood had been foreseen as early as the 1950s by the ANC, namely that the violence of the apartheid regime would eventually drive South African people to resort to violence themselves in self-defence.

We questioned them particularly about the possibility of a suspension of violence on both sides leading towards cessation. The ANC's response was that it was important to understand the nature of the violence, how it came about, who started it and how the others had reacted. The introduction of apartheid in 1948 had heralded an era of unprecedented violence by the South African State. The ANC's response had been to counteract Government-sponsored violence with a campaign of non-violence which had been pursued throughout the 1950s, despite the employment of increased violence by the South African Government to restrict the ANC and to stifle black rights. This culminated at the end of the 1950s with Sharpeville and a calamitous decade of killing.

Still the ANC persisted with its policy of non-violence. It was only in 1961, when the army was deployed in a massive way, nationwide, to stamp out a peaceful strike organized by Nelson Mandela, that the ANC decided that it was necessary to embark on an armed struggle. Despite this, over the past twenty years or so the ANC said it had been very selective in its targets and the number of deaths resulting from ANC activities was hardly twenty. In one single incident in Soweto about a thousand children were shot at indiscriminately by the security forces.

Violence in South Africa was attributed as being the result of an apartheid system which needed guns, arrests and prisons to maintain it; violence would abate if the system was dismantled. With the abandonment of apartheid the way would open for a cessation of violence on both sides. If the army and the police pulled out of the townships, the ANC could begin to consider a suspension of violence.

In any event the ANC's stand on violence did not mean there could not be serious negotiation. There were many instances of negotiation taking place to end hostilities, as had been the case in Zimbabwe. There were other cases directly involving the South African Government in negotiation in the midst of conflict and fighting, as in Mozambique and Angola. If the conditions set out in the Nassau Accord were fulfilled by the South African Government and if there were seen to be prospects for resolving fundamental issues within a short period, it would go a long way in demonstrating that there was no need for violence and help to reduce the level of the armed struggle. It was conceivable that the struggle could be called off altogether. But before that stage was reached the ANC could hardly be expected to act unilaterally. For the ANC to renounce violence now would be to reduce itself to a state of helplessness. There must first be sufficient indications of the South African Government's readiness to negotiate the transition to non-racial sovereignty.

The ANC counselled us against being drawn into a situation with the Government where, as with the Contact Group on Namibia, there were continually postponed decisions and deferred expectations. Its assessment was that the South African Government's declarations of reform had shown no evidence of a preparedness to undertake the fundamental changes that were being demanded. There had been no real departures in policy, only an attempt to lull opposition forces into inactivity and to consolidate white minority rule. In the circumstances, we were urged to adhere to our six-month timetable and not be drawn into playing a game in which it would appear that the South

African Government was beginning a process and at the same time allowing time to slip by. By taking a firm stand and adhering to our timetable the real intentions of the South African Government in respect of negotiations would be tested.

THE PAN-AFRICANIST CONGRESS OF AZANIA (PAC)

The PAC viewed the present conflict in South Africa as entirely due to the persistence of apartheid. The Commonwealth Accord had laid down five steps that should be taken 'in a genuine manner and as a matter of urgency' by the Government. After six months the Government had not addressed itself to any of them.

In the PAC view, the possibility of a relatively peaceful and negotiated settlement in South Africa depended entirely upon the Government. If the Government decided to abolish apartheid and accept true democracy in a unified South Africa, peace would prevail overnight. But it would be politically naïve to believe at this point in time that the Government had come round to abandoning white supremacy. The struggle and the pressures against it would therefore need to be intensified.

They considered that in respect of violence there were at least two types, structural and direct violence, and the South African Government was guilty of both. In the PAC view the question of violence did not arise for the oppressed and unarmed majority in South Africa; their acts were a form of self-defence. If the Government addressed itself to the problem of violence convincingly, there would be an adequate and positive response from the PAC. As a movement committed to the genuine liberation of the South African people, the PAC was primarily concerned to ensure that the momentum of opposition was sustained, that international pressures were increased and that the fighting capacity of the people was enlarged – unless they could be convinced otherwise with tangible proof.

In respect of negotiations, the PAC would be willing to participate in talks but would insist that there were only two contending forces – the racist regime and its collaborators, such as 'Bantustan leaders and Tricameral puppets', and the oppressed people. Inkatha's collaboration had served the

Government's goal of dividing the opposition in a variety of ways, some obvious and others more subtle.

THE UNITED DEMOCRATIC FRONT (UDF), COSATU AND AZAPO

Within South Africa itself, we sought out all the principal individuals and organizations who could help us to judge the mood of the country's black people and whose thinking would be relevant to any process of negotiation. Among the principal personalities that we met were Mrs Winnie Mandela, Dr Allan Boesak and Bishop Desmond Tutu. Among the organizations, the UDF, the Congress of South African Trade Unions (COSATU) and the Azanian People's Organization (AZAPO) merited particular attention. We also established contact with community bodies like Black Sash and the Detainees' Parents' Support Committee. We received unstinting help and co-operation from them all.

That this proved to be the case was by no means a foregone conclusion. For example, prior to the Group's visit to South Africa, the UDF had decided at national level not to co-operate with the Group. There was suspicion not just in the UDF but in other quarters as well that the Group as conceived at Nassau was designed to give the Government a breathing space, to provide an opportunity for staving off pressures for fundamental change and to diminish the momentum of the internal struggle. A careful and delicate process of personal contacts and discussions was necessary to explain the Group's true purport and role.

Nor was this the only difficulty. In the absence of conditions of political freedom, it was by no means easy for organizations to consult with their own members or to arrange meetings involving their collective leadership. For example, prominent UDF members and office bearers had been arrested and placed under banning orders (under the Security Act and the emergency legislation) or otherwise harassed to the point where they could only operate covertly or under subterfuge.

Our conversations with the individuals and organizations mentioned above had two essential purposes: first, to gain a better appreciation of the situation on the ground and second, to understand their attitude to negotiations.

The UDF is the largest country-wide political movement in South Africa. A coalition of more than six hundred groups throughout the land, it is non-racial and welcomes whites to its fold. COSATU is a powerful force in and beyond the industrial arena and commands a membership of 500,000. The political influence of both is clearly far greater than that of AZAPO. There are also differences between the UDF and AZAPO. Nevertheless, if we present their views as a composite, it is simply to emphasize, in terms of our own mandate, the substantial commonality of the views expressed to us. We highlight the most relevant aspects.

● Almost without exception, the Government was regarded as deceitful and untrustworthy, a past master of 'double-think' and 'double-speak'. Its word could not be believed. In any case, the country was now looking for deeds, not words.
● A huge credibility gap existed which would somehow have to be bridged if there was to be negotiation.
● The Government's programme of reforms was dismissed as too little too late, essentially a cosmetic exercise intended to placate international opinion, while at the same time sustaining Government by a white clique. Far from dismantling apartheid, it preserved all its essentials.
● It was then not for the Government unilaterally to take decisions and then expect the rest of the country to fall in line. How could apartheid be reformed? It had to be ended. This was what the struggle in South Africa was all about.
● If there were to be negotiations, they could only be on a realistic and principled foundation – a firm commitment of intent by the Government to negotiate a non-racial constitution. The Tricameral Constitution would have to be scrapped along with all other puppet bodies created under the Black Local Authorities Act and other instruments of racist rule. Was the Government prepared to start from a negotiating position free from ethnic

and racial overtones? There was scepticism whether the Government was ready to make such a 'quantum' leap.

● On the issue of violence, a harrowing picture was presented of Government repression and police brutality. We were told that the Government was conscious that the situation was slipping out of its control, and had therefore intensified its acts of terror on the people. Funerals were being disrupted and tear-gas, sjamboks and bullets used on innocent people. Inter-black violence was being fomented as a pretext for keeping the troops in the townships. For the black people, it was no longer a question of self-defence, but of survival. They would continue to resist this onslaught with all their strength.

● If the Government was serious in its professed desire to find a peaceful solution to the country's problems, it must unambiguously commit itself to dismantle apartheid, end its war on the people by withdrawing all troops from the townships, create conditions of political freedom and release political prisoners. It must negotiate only with those who had the standing and authority to speak on behalf of the people.

It was clear to us that these were the views of dominant sections of black opinion with extensive grassroots support. They were articulated to us by African, coloured, Indian and white; the young and the old; the famous and the humble; men and women. All, however, claimed to share one objective – a nonracial South Africa – and one experience – harassment by the Government. At one of our meetings, three participants between them had served over 60 years on Robben Island. To us, they appeared persons of goodwill who would have graced any normal society, bent only on the ultimate good of South Africa.

PROGRESSIVE FEDERAL PARTY (PFP)

The PFP is the principal Opposition Party in the white House of Assembly. Its leader, Dr Van Zyl Slabbert, had resigned from Parliament shortly before our first visit to South Africa. We did, however, meet with Mr Colin Eglin, the new opposition leader and some of his party colleagues.

We were told that although there was a general loosening in the apartheid system, it was far from being dismantled. On a charitable view the Government appeared unsure as to what was meant by dismantling apartheid. The fundamental problem was that the Constitution itself embodied apartheid.

The PFP forms an important part of that common ground of opinion which calls for the ending of apartheid, the release of political prisoners, the withdrawal of troops from the townships and the permitting of free political activity as a means of generating the confidence necessary to persuade people to negotiate. It perceived a widening gap between the Government and the governed and expressed alarm at the increasing violence on all sides.

THE 'HOMELANDS'

No Commonwealth country recognizes the so-called 'homeland'. We were left in no doubt that the 'homeland' system is anathema to the majority of black people, who reject it as part and parcel of the apartheid system.

Nevertheless, because the 'homelands' are part of the South African reality, and Chief Mangosuthu Buthelezi is an important political figure in his own right, the Group met a selected number of 'homeland' leaders – Chief Buthelezi, Chief Minister of KwaZulu; Chief Mabuza, Chief Minister of KwaNgwane; and the 'Foreign and Manpower Ministers' of Bophuthatswana.

We recognized the differences in views and status in and between the individual 'homeland' leaders. We questioned the Ministers of the 'independent' Bophuthatswana closely about the consistency of their own position in professing to oppose apartheid, yet purporting to be a 'sovereign' state not recognized by any Government other than South Africa; and their part in support of what was universally interpreted as a retrograde step against the interest of a non-racial, democratic and united South African State.

We acknowledged the special place of Chief Buthelezi, who described the policies of the South African Government as being founded on ethnicity and based on the principle of divide and rule. He believed this to be the major source of disunity among blacks which, he said, had the making of a civil war. He had rejected 'independence' as he believed such states were the creation of apartheid and fuelled division between the blacks. There was need for reconciliation not only between blacks, but between blacks and whites. It was for this reason that he stressed the importance of plans for the unified administration of KwaNatal in which he was now heavily involved.

In Chief Buthelezi's view, Nelson Mandela was integral to a solution of the situation. If he were released, violence could be defused. In fact, if Mr Mandela, in a democratic South Africa, were elected by the majority, he would be ready and willing to serve under him.

He endorsed the conditions spelt out in the Nassau Accord as the minimum that the Government should do to encourage the process of dialogue. In addition, three other conditions were necessary without which dialogue could not start: the repeal of the Group Areas Act; the repeal of the Population Registration Act; and the guarantee of freedom of association.

THE BUSINESS COMMUNITY

We recognized in the South African business community potential for exerting pressures upon the Government to the benefit of the country as a whole. A number of businessmen, individually and on behalf of their corporations, had been on record in calling for radical change in the apartheid system. Business leaders on the whole believed that the prosperity of the country depended upon achieving improvements in black purchasing power and the creation of more skilled jobs for blacks. The predominant need was to strike a viable balance between political desiderata and economic reality. There were strong pressures in play – high black unemployment, a stretched economy, disinvestment, and increasing white emigration. Political repression and violence should give way to the broadening of political freedom and genuine black participation in governing

John Malecela and Ted Scott with the Rev. Abe Visagie at De Aar, in the centre of the Midlands. (Photo: Hugh Craft)

Swaran Singh in Soweto. Members of the Group walk through Port Elizabeth's Black township. (Photo: Malcolm Fraser)

Black feet on white sand. General Obasanjo on a 'white only' beach at Port Elizabeth. His widely publicized walk with Malcolm Fraser hastened desegregation of the beach. (Photo: Malcolm Fraser)

Dancing in the streets! John Malecela and General Obasanjo join in a dance of welcome by volunteer roadside workers in Hanover. Official administration had collapsed. (Photo: Jeremy Pope)

South Africa. There was a clear preference for dealing with 'moderate' blacks who held out the best hope for a peaceful and prosperous future. The political negotiating process would be difficult and protracted, but the Group had a role to play as a catalyst in promoting credible interaction in South Africa towards genuine negotiation.

Our clear impression was that the business community was seeking peaceful reform along the middle-ground but was, to some extent, out of touch with black opinion. We expressed the view that they could and should exert greater pressure on the Government.

THE CHURCHES

We sought the views of the church. We did so believing that the church with its extensive grassroots contacts and intimate knowledge of the problems and difficulties of ordinary people, would be an accurate barometer of the popular mood.

We found the church, while experiencing external tensions, was – with one or two exceptions – a force for change. This applied both to the leadership and the laity, to the cities and townships as well as the rural areas. At the parish level we spoke to clergy who in normal circumstances would have been content to pursue their pastoral duties, but now found themselves compelled to speak out against injustice and racism because of their pastoral concern for people. In so doing they had suffered along with their people – detention and trial, misrepresentation and harassment, threats and injury. Church buildings have become almost the only sure refuge for freedom of expression and interracial association, and even their sanctity is at times periodically violated.

The leaders of the South African Council of Churches (SACC), the umbrella organization covering the major Protestant denominations, and of the South African Catholic Bishops Conference (SACBC) showed considerable identity of view over the central issues. They shared a deep-seated fear that South Africa stood on the brink of catastrophe and hoped that the Commonwealth initiative could play a decisive role in securing peace. They particularly deplored the growing incidence of police brutality and harassment in the black townships which extended even to funerals where police presence was highly provocative and resulted in fuelling wide-scale violence.

The Government's reform programme was regarded essentially as leaving the fundamentals untouched. They were critical of the Government's tendency in one breath to speak of South Africa as 'one nation' and in the next to talk of its tribal heterogeneity. The reform programme was no more than titivation with the apartheid system, leaving blacks worse off than they had been in 1948 when, in theory at least, they had all possessed South African citizenship.

To avoid the otherwise inevitable bloodbath and to build confidence across the full spectrum of society, the SACC and SACBC believed that the Government should declare publicly its intention not merely to reform, but to dismantle apartheid within a specific time-frame. The emergence of an undivided nation in which everyone was recognized as a South African citizen, possessed basic political rights and enjoyed freedom of movement without impediment, was the objective.

It was agreed that to generate and sustain a climate in which political dialogue might prosper, the South African Government would have to meet the basic prerequisites outlined in the Nassau Accord – the withdrawal of troops from townships, the release of Nelson Mandela and other political detainees, the unbanning of political organizations and the return of political exiles. Such measures would attract positive responses from political bodies and from the disenchanted youth, and would contribute towards the ending of violence. If the Government failed to take these steps, violence would continue.

The church had an active role to play in the education and reconciliation process. Whilst the churches would not condone violence, they feared that people's patience was wearing dangerously thin and violence appeared to many as the only avenue left. People on all sides and of all colours were afraid and needed reassurance.

By contrast, in the several sections of the Dutch Reformed Church (DRC), originally the theological and philosophical cornerstone of the structures of apartheid, we found one section of the white church still clinging to apartheid philosophy. In its view the entrenchment of separate development was necessary to harmonize the collective contribution of all racial groups to the nation. Separate development, it contended, was to the common and individual good as long as individual human dignity was not damaged. While we were in South Africa its Synod reaffirmed a 'white only' position. However, both the other two white sections of the church criticized this action on theological grounds, while the covenant church (originally the coloured section of the DRC) and the black section of the DRC are giving courageous leadership in the struggle against apartheid, both theologically and politically. We conveyed to representatives of the pro-apartheid white Dutch Reformed Church our conviction, based on our personal observation, that they were blinkered to the realities of their own country and failing to give leadership to members of their church, many of whom occupy important government positions, in reading the signs of the times. We also pointed out to Government leaders that although South Africa claims by constitution to be a Christian country, the church worldwide challenges its apartheid policies on theological grounds and holds the Government accountable to Christian values.

Overview

The Group was forcibly struck by the overwhelming desire in the country for a non-violent negotiated settlement. The onus rested on the Government, as the wielders of police and military power, to introduce a climate in which negotiation involving all sections of political opinion could take place on a basis of equality without let, hindrance or fear of harassment. People from all walks of life were distraught at the level of violence which had become commonplace. There were positively identifiable problems and a striking identity of views on solutions. What reforms had been introduced so far or were promised were insufficient, and were widely interpreted as ploys to gain time or as surface ripples on the deep waters of apartheid. A clear, unequivocal statement of intent by the Government to introduce positive confidence-building measures and action in that direction would go a long way to restoring people's faith in the sincerity and bona fides of the Government and attract people to the negotiating forum. Anything less would amount to opting for the perpetuation of violence and the wholesale bloodbath which many saw on the horizon.

Chapter 6
The Group's Proposals

At the conclusion of our consultations we felt satisfied that we had, within the time available to us, consulted on the widest possible basis with all appropriate groups and individuals in South Africa – from the State President and senior Cabinet Ministers to displaced poverty-stricken refugees and squatters; from business magnates, prelates and members of the church and university dons, to industrial and agricultural workers; from political prisoners, exiles and prominent dissidents to ordinary people wanting only the best for their children and future generations. We had come to listen, to observe, and to explore in an open manner. Our perceptions and impressions derived not only from talking but from first-hand experience in the urban and rural areas in many parts of the country.

We were satisfied that the ground existed on the basis of which a negotiated solution to South Africa's problems could be attempted if there was the necessary political will among all concerned. No serious person we met was interested in a fight to the finish; all favoured negotiations and peaceful solutions.

We drew the conclusions that in dealing with the question of violence, lack of confidence and credibility constituted major obstacles; that the Government's programme of 'reforms' was insufficient and would not end apartheid; that the initiative for progress rested, in the first instance, with the Government; that a special role devolved upon the ANC; and that if a major conflagration was to be averted time was running out.

In conveying this view to Ministers, the Group expressed its conviction that to build the credibility necessary to enter a negotiating situation, it would be essential for the Government to concentrate on a comprehensive 'package' of proposals designed specifically to elicit a positive response from the black leadership. A piecemeal approach that addressed peripheral issues of apartheid would not satisfy black aspirations. A 'package' of measures dealing with major grievances could, however, trigger the positive response from black leaders that the Government assured us it so earnestly sought.

On this basis we put forward proposals to the Government which we believed would enable negotiations to commence. It was clear to us that a number of elements would have to be encompassed within these proposals if they were to stand any chance of acceptance.

The first related to the negotiating agenda in its broadest sense. What were negotiations to be about or designed to achieve? Despite the Government's various statements that apartheid was outmoded, the ANC and black opinion within the country was looking for a more positive declaration of intent and some specific and meaningful steps in regard to the dismantling of the apartheid system. The reforms implemented so far had not impressed the black community; there was thus a need for the Government to make a firmer and more categorical statement of intent.

The second major element would need to be confidence-building measures to allay suspicions and fears and to demonstrate the Government's good faith. There would be need for a major act of reconciliation – the release of all political prisoners, with a view to creating a new climate in the country.

The third element would be a link between the release of political prisoners and the initiation of a political process. Little purpose would be served by freeing Nelson Mandela and others if the parties to which they belonged remained unable to function. The corollary of their release must therefore be the establishment of political freedom and the recognition of those rights of free speech and assembly which had for so long been denied. This would also be essential for the black community to give their leaders the mandate and legitimacy they would need to make the negotiating process meaningful.

The fourth element would need to be a moratorium on violence – by both the Government and its opponents. On the part of the Government, this would require a suspension of the practice of detaining its opponents without trial; the withdrawal of the security forces from the townships, whose presence and conduct we had seen and had ample reason to believe were provocative and inflammatory; these and other elements would be matched by a suspension of violence by the ANC and others.

The fifth element would need to be synchronization. The Government and the ANC were each looking to the other to make the first move. We believed the only way this problem could be resolved would be through prior agreement between both to act simultaneously in fulfilment of their respective commitments.

It was on this basis that we developed what we described as a 'Possible Negotiating Concept'. It embodied the 'package' approach which we believe to be necessary. Its preamble constituted a firm statement of intent that apartheid would be ended; its operative paragraph set out measures that were needed to create a climate of confidence and enable all concerned to turn to the task of constructing a new South Africa; and the postscript embodied statements made by the South African Government which we hoped would facilitate the negotiating process.

The text of the 'Possible Negotiating Concept' was as follows:

The South African Government has declared its commitment to dismantling the system of apartheid, to ending racial discrimination and to broad-based negotiations leading to new constitutional arrangements for power-sharing by all the people of South Africa. In the light of preliminary and as yet incomplete discussions with representatives of various organizations and groups, within and outside South Africa, we believe that in the context of specific and meaningful steps being taken towards ending apartheid, the following additional action might ensure negotiations and a break in the cycle of violence.

On the part of the Government:

(a) Removal of the military from the townships, providing for freedom of assembly and discussion and suspension of detention without trial.

(b) The release of Nelson Mandela and other political prisoners and detainees.

(c) The unbanning of the ANC and PAC and the permitting of normal political activity.

On the part of the ANC and others:

Entering negotiations and suspending violence.

It is our view that simultaneous announcements incorporating these ideas might be negotiated if the Government were to be interested in pursuing this broad approach.

In the light of the Government's indication to us that it:

(i) is not in principle against the release of Nelson Mandela and similar prisoners;

(ii) is not opposed in principle to the unbanning of any organizations;

(iii) is prepared to enter into negotiations with the acknowledged leaders of the people of South Africa;

(iv) is committed to removal of discrimination, not only from the statute books but also from South African society as a whole;

(v) is committed to ending of white domination;

(vi) will not prescribe who may represent black communities in negotiations on a new constitution for South Africa;

(vii) is prepared to negotiate on an open agenda;

the South African Government may wish to give serious consideration to the approach outlined in this note.

The concept was transmitted to the Minister for Constitutional Development and Planning, Mr Heunis, and to Foreign Minister Pik Botha under cover of letters dated 13 March which stated our belief that it offers 'a real chance of establishing productive negotiations about the future of South Africa'. If the Government believed that there was some future role for the Group we stood 'ready to advance the course of negotiations'.

In our discussions the previous day with Minister Heunis and Foreign Minister Botha, we had stressed that the concept had evolved out of our consultations and our judgement of what might be possible. We had not shown it to the ANC, and we were not operating on a mandate from any outside group or groups. In formulating the concept, we had juxtaposed the Government's own assurances to the Group alongside those demands of the black community which in our view, represented an irreducible and reasonable minimum if negotiations were to be possible. We further explained that we had engaged in some hard talk with those whose demands had been unrealistic and with others who wanted to inject conditions or views into a pre-negotiating stage which were essentially agenda items for the negotiations themselves.

We emphasized that an immediate response from the Government was being sought, but we hoped the Government would consider the concept as a whole. If it saw no merit in our proposals, little purpose would be served by taking them to the other relevant parties inside and outside South Africa.

Our proposal that all political prisoners be released – an essential part of the concept – was questioned by the Government on the grounds that the term 'political prisoner' was incapable of precise definition. However we had no doubt that this difficulty could be overcome if the Government had the will.

In South Africa, the political trial is characterized by the denial of various rights enjoyed by ordinary accused persons including denials of access to a lawyer before being charged; indefinite detention with no right to be brought before the court; denial of bail on the say-so of a political officer (the Attorney-General) overriding any decision by a judicial officer; allowing a person to be charged for a second time, after acquittal, for a different offence arising out of the same conduct; compelling witnesses to incriminate themselves; and in some cases requiring an accused to establish his innocence 'beyond a reasonable doubt'.

In these, and other ways, what one writer has described as 'a highly discriminatory set of rules of procedure' have been constructed for South Africa's political trials, that 'seriously undermines the value of the political trial as a process of judicial authentication.' It also makes grave inroads upon individual liberty by seriously eroding essential procedural safeguards. It would follow, logically, that any prisoner convicted under such a biased and imbalanced procedure should be regarded as being a 'political prisoner'.

Beyond this, however, we believe it is a relatively simple matter to identify persons who are 'political prisoners', namely, those for whom, whatever the circumstances of their original imprisonment, continuing confinement is now wholly a political act and bearing no relationship to the needs and objectives of the criminal justice system.

On 24 April 1986, Foreign Minister Botha replied to us saying that his Government continued 'to believe that the Group could serve a useful purpose' and accordingly proposed a further exchange of views 'particularly on the modalities of achieving a suspension of violence and facilitating discussions'. The full text of that reply follows:

Dear Mr Fraser and General Obasanjo

The South African Government has been giving serious consideration to the salient features of the 'possible negotiating concept' attached to your letter of 13 March 1986 which I have been asked to respond to.

You will be aware, from previous statements which the South African State President and other members of the South African Government have made on the issue of the release of Mr Nelson Mandela, that the South African Government's basic concern is that his release should not be accompanied by or result in further violence.

It must be clear that the key to the release of Mr Mandela and similar prisoners, withdrawal of the Security Forces from certain urban areas and lifting of the ban on the ANC and PAC is a suspension of violence.

The question which arises is how this can be put into effect. In your 'possible negotiating concept' you suggest that, 'in the context of specific and meaningful steps being taken towards ending apartheid', certain additional action by the South African Government and the ANC and others might ensure negotiations and a break in the cycle of violence. Moreover you will recall that during the Group's recent discussions with representatives of the South African Government, the influx control system and pass laws were highlighted by the Group as important issues affecting the daily lives of black people. At that stage the Group was aware of the State President's commitment, made during the opening of Parliament earlier this year, that this situation would be fundamentally altered by 1 July 1986. In line with this commitment the State President announced in Parliament on Friday 18 April 1986, that no further charges would be preferred in terms of the existing legislation; that people who have been convicted in terms of this legislation would be released forthwith, and that those who are being detained pending trial would likewise be released. The Government proposed to repeal or amend no fewer than 34 Acts and Proclamations to ensure that the movement of people will not be subject to discrimination on the grounds of colour or race.

These additional reform measures testify to the Government's acceptance that no further forced removals in pursuit of a political ideology will take place. The Government has noted with satisfaction in this connection the Group's recognition that positive actions on the part of the South African Government should be matched by corresponding responses by those now opposed to negotiations and committed to violence.

The Commonwealth Group of Eminent Persons will understand that if the South African Government does not move along the lines suggested in its 'possible negotiating concept' and violence continues or increases, the Government may have no alternative but to take appropriate measures to control the violence. The Group will recall that I raised this issue with them during their visit. It is my recollection that it responded that it recognized the responsibility of the Government to maintain order but the question arises whether such action on the part of the Government would not then result in further punitive action against South Africa. This is a most important issue which will require further discussion.

The South African Government continues to believe that the Group can serve a useful purpose and it accordingly proposes, in the light of the foregoing, that the whole Group or representative members of the Group meet with representatives of the South African Government to exchange views on how further to proceed, particularly on the modalities of achieving a suspension of violence and facilitating discussions.

Yours sincerely
(Signed) R. F. Botha

In considering this reply, which the South African Ambassador in London assured us should be regarded as positive, we focused on a number of issues in the context of the Government's selective comments.

Our concept had looked to specific and meaningful steps being taken by the South African Government towards ending apartheid: the response seemed to imply that the Government had already done what was required of it, in that it seemed to believe that such action could be confined to changes relating to the movement of persons resulting from the termination of influx control.

In addition to the action to be taken by the Government towards ending apartheid, our concept had envisaged additional action necessary to ensure negotiations and a break in the cycle of violence. These specific elements of the concept appeared to have been treated lightly in the Minister's reply. For example:

● it projected a withdrawal of security forces from some black townships only;
● there was no mention of measures to provide for political freedoms and the suspension of detention without trial;
● a reference to the release of Nelson Mandela and similar prisoners seemed to imply that the Government did not envisage the release of all prisoners and detainees on political charges;
● and it was not clear whether the broad-based negotiations leading to new constitutional arrangements for power-sharing by all the people of South Africa outside the present racist structures, as envisaged in our concept, were the kind of negotiations being contemplated by the Government.

The Minister's letter also raised a proposition (later conveyed by the State President to the Tokyo meeting of the seven industrial country leaders in May) that economic sanctions should not be imposed on South Africa should there be a breakdown in the suspension of violence during a negotiating period.

There seemed, however, to be some positive aspects to the Minister's reply, one of which we interpreted as an important concession by the South African Government. Instead of demanding the renunciation of violence as a precondition for talks, the Government was now prepared to contemplate the term adopted in our concept, the 'suspension' of violence. This repeated the term used in the State President's first letter to us of 24 December and appeared to represent significant progress towards getting the parties to the table. The reply also referred to 'lifting of the ban on the ANC and PAC' in a manner that seemed worthy of further exploration.

Encouraged by the contents and tone of the Government's reponse, we agreed to return to South Africa for a further round of discussions during which we would press for a more specific response to our negotiating concept. The text of our reply on 1 May 1986 was as follows:

My dear Foreign Minister,

Thank you for your letter of 24 April 1986 whose contents we have noted with care.

We are encouraged that the South African Government sees constructive possibilities in the negotiating concept which we left with you and Minister Heunis at the conclusion of our visit to South Africa and by the continuing role that we might be able to play in its furtherance. Mindful of the value of a more precise understanding of the position of your Government if real progress is to be made towards negotiation, it will be our endeavour to seek this during our next round of discussions in Southern Africa. We therefore welcome your invitation to come to Cape Town.

Arising from your letter, there are a number of important issues which require further discussion. We will want to take the opportunity to deliberate with you on these in furtherance of our mandate. We recognize that your letter highlights only some aspects of our own thinking and approach; these, of course, remain as set out in our negotiating concept, and elaborated more fully during our conversations with the South African Government.

We much appreciate the opportunity we have had to begin the process of clarification in our conversations with Mr von Hirschberg in London today. He has pinpointed your concerns on the question of violence, among others; we have drawn attention to the issues in our negotiating concept on which we will be seeking a more specific response. Mr von Hirschberg will no doubt be reporting the details of these conversations to you. It is our belief that the best assurance against further measures by the international community, to which you refer, would be the early commencement and assiduous pursuit of genuine negotiations along the lines envisaged in our negotiating concept and involving the authentic leaders of the people of South Africa. We earnestly hope that, at the time of the Group's forthcoming visit to South Africa, it will be possible to clarify all these matters in a manner which will enable the process to be carried forward speedily on the basis of understanding and agreement among all concerned.

We looked forward to seeing you again on 13 May.

Yours sincerely,
Signed
Malcolm Fraser   Olusegun Obasanjo

We resumed our discussions in South Africa with Foreign

Minister Botha on 13 May and met a group of eight senior Ministers of the Cabinet's Constitutional Committee under the chairmanship of Minister Heunis on 19 May. At this stage the Government had had the concept for nine weeks.

The chronology of events during our return visit to South Africa is described sequentially, highlighting matters of particular relevance.

Tuesday, 13 May: Meeting with Foreign Minister Pik Botha

The discussion centered on two principal matters. The first related to what Nelson Mandela had said to us on our previous visit and the South African Government's understanding that he was not interested in negotiations but only in a transfer of power. This had been reinforced by a statement made by his Attorney some time ago as well as by Mrs Winnie Mandela's recent remarks about liberating the country. The Government believed that these statements derived from, and reflected, Mr Mandela's own thinking. There were thus inconsistencies in what Mr Mandela had told the Group (and Opposition MP Mrs Helen Suzman) and the continuing ANC campaign of violence. Some way must be found to establish the true position of the ANC and Nelson Mandela himself.

The second related to the situation on the ground. The Government could not take what were, in effect, irreversible decisions and steps towards negotiations unless these were preceded by some tangible, visible evidence of a de-escalation of violence. The Government believed that the violence was perpetrated by the ANC which was communist-dominated. Under no circumstances would the Government allow a Marxist takeover of the country. He had no mandate to enter into negotiations with the ANC.

We were immediately concerned that the Minister was going back to the positions implicit in his letter of 24 April. Instead of dealing with specific elements in the concept and the 'modalities' of its implementation, he had raised a number of entirely new issues. His remarks suggested a hardening of the Government's position towards the ANC on the basis of which it would be prepared to negotiate.

Wednesday, 14 May: Meeting with Minister of Justice, Mr S. Coetsee

At the meeting with Minister Coetsee it was confirmed that the Government had agreed to our request for a second, longer meeting with Nelson Mandela. We would be allowed such a meeting in Pollsmoor Prison the following day. The Government, it was made clear, saw value in eliciting Mr Mandela's position on the issue of violence as a means of securing political change. The Minister reflected on the consequences that might follow Mr Mandela's unconditional release. We reiterated our view that Nelson Mandela was a man of integrity and that his release would contribute significantly to the prospects for a de-escalation of violence and viable negotiations. The Minister informed us that the State President would be making an important speech the following afternoon that might have a bearing on our work.

Thursday, 15 May: State President's Speech to the President's Council

The State President's address, broadcast nationwide, spelled out the principles that were to guide the Government in its move towards 'a new constitutional dispensation'. An important feature was a list of 'non-negotiables' (Annex VIII) on which the Government would insist in any negotiated solution.

We read some significance into the fact that the speech had been delivered whilst we were in South Africa, and that it warned specifically against interference by outside bodies. The structure and tenor of the speech seemed to indicate the emergence of a harder posture at the highest level. The emphasis on a rejection and renunciation of violence suggested a return by the Government to its original position. At the time it was possible to interpret this speech as sending a message to the Government's own right wing. Later events showed otherwise.

Friday, 16 May: Meeting with Nelson Mandela

We took the opportunity to brief Mr Mandela on progress in our work and consultations to date and shared the negotiating concept with him. Though we emphasized that an immediate response from him was not being sought, Mr Mandela volunteered that he had no difficulty in accepting the concept as a starting point – but he emphasized that he was responding as an individual in the isolation of prison and that it was important for the Group to have the reaction of the ANC. In order to arrive at a more considered view it was imperative that arrangements should be made for him to consult with his ANC colleagues both in Pollsmoor and on Robben Island as well as with other influential figures within South Africa. The ANC in Lusaka would want to take these internal views into account.

Nelson Mandela confirmed his desire to see violence end and to see peaceful conditions prevail so that fruitful discussions could be held between black leaders and the Government. He reiterated his belief that the violence could be controlled. The Government knew of his commitment to help in that. But his release would not be enough – the prior understanding as envisaged in the concept between the ANC and the Government on the steps to be taken, including the withdrawal of the security forces from the townships, would be essential. It would also be necessary to ensure that he and his colleagues could move freely around the country using their persuasive powers to create a condition of calm in which the agreed negotiating process could begin.

We put these propositions to Ministers. Had the Government been serious about initiating negotiations in peaceful conditions in the country, we believe that it would have facilitated the process of consultation that Mr Mandela was seeking with his ANC colleagues and other black leaders in the country.

Friday, 16 May: Meeting with Foreign Minister Pik Botha

We reported to Foreign Minister Botha the outcome of our discussions with Mr Mandela viz. that he had reasserted his commitment to work towards an end of violence and his desire for talks with the Government; that his release would enable him to use his influence to bring about a de-escalation of violence; and that as an individual he endorsed the negotiating concept as an acceptable starting point but would need to consult with his ANC colleagues to obtain a considered ANC view. We urged the Government to permit this process of consultation to start.

We understood from the Minister that the Government had not accepted the concept, nor had it rejected it. The meeting set down for the following Monday with the Constitutional Committee of the Cabinet would be important in making progess. He raised what he perceived as the major problems of the South African Government with the concept.

The Government did not see itself as dealing with one party only, specifically the ANC. There were many parties in South Africa whose principal objective was to unseat the Government. All must be involved in any future negotiating process. The question of detention without trial, one of the proposals contained in the negotiating concept, would provide the South African Government with special problems in that it involved legislation. All its other proposals were capable of being achieved without introducing any law. (We were unable to appreciate this reasoning, as we had not asked for a repeal of the Government's preventive detention powers, only that they be held in abeyance.) But detention without trial was necessary for the Government to control lawlessness and disorder wherever it surfaced and without distinction on the grounds of colour.

A further point related to questions centering around the issue of violence. He questioned the term 'suspension' of violence as it appeared in the concept (and the Accord). The Government's understanding was that this meant a cessation, an end for all time. If the notion was that violence could be resumed because of differences at the conference table, then the Commonwealth initiative stood no chance of success. Additionally there needed to be some evidence of a de-escalation of violence prior to negotiations getting under way. Another obvious difficulty for the Government would arise if the release of Mr Mandela was to be accompanied by a sudden upsurge of violence.

We explained that although not articulated in our concept, but implicit in it, was the expectation that the black leadership would issue a joint appeal for calm. Thereafter each leader would lend his personal efforts to bring about and sustain conditions conducive to peaceful political activity. In particular, we saw a special role for Nelson Mandela in this regard. We expressed our conviction that the standing of the principal black leaders in the townships would enable them to give effect to a suspension of violence.

The Minister emphasized that the Government held power and was determined to govern. There were only three ways to remove the Government: through white votes, by violence, or by negotiations to herald a new era. In respect of its own constituents, the Government viewed with concern the emergence of reactionary right-wing elements. He asserted strongly, however, that it was not possible to topple the Government either by internal violence or by external pressure – the Government could generate enormous military power. But he saw no point in anyone pursuing the violent route especially when a negotiated solution was, in the final analysis, inevitable.

Saturday, 17 May: Meeting with ANC representatives in Lusaka

We travelled to Lusaka to brief the ANC leadership on progress and to share the negotiating concept with them. We reported that the concept had been with the Government for more than two months and that we had deliberately not revealed it to the ANC until this juncture because we had seen little point in discussing it with them prior to receiving positive indications from the Government. The Government, while indicating that it was considering it seriously, had not yet said either 'yes' or 'no'. Its acceptance would involve the Government in doing a great deal to prove its sincerity and genuineness in wanting a negotiated solution. Our consultations with Nelson Mandela had been extensive but he had emphasized that in reacting favourably to the concept as a starting point he was speaking as an individual. He had stressed that, if there was to be a considered reaction from him, it would be necessary for him to consult with his ANC colleagues. We informed them that we had urged strongly upon the Government that Mr Mandela's proposal for consultations with fellow ANC prisoners and others inside the country be allowed.

Mr Tambo, ANC President, said it was not going to be possible to give a considered response straight away. He noted that the South African Government, after all these weeks, had still not given the Group a substantive answer. The ANC was in a far more difficult position than the Government. It was based in Lusaka in exile; the organization was spread out; it had responsibilities to many people, including leaders in jail and all those within South Africa who supported its endeavours and influenced its thinking.

By way of initial reaction, however, he was in a position to say that in so far as the concept corresponded to the principles and requirements of the Nassau Accord, it would command the support of the ANC.

Mr Tambo said the ANC had no objection to negotiations and would participate in them so long as they were proper and honest, and not just a device to quell internal demands and weaken external pressures. The ANC could never forget that they were dealing with a regime which did not honour its undertakings and was a master of prevarication. When the South African Government said it wanted negotiations the question arose whether it was honest in its intentions. Had Pretoria not negotiated with the South West African People's Organization (SWAPO) and the Contact Group for eight long years? Had it not negotiated with Mozambique and Angola and signed agreements which it had then proceeded to violate from the very outset?

There was thus a need for the South African Government to demonstrate its good faith, and for the Group to apply the acid test to satisfy itself that the Government was ready for negotiations. No negotiations could be fruitful if there were the slightest reservations in the mind of the Government about the dismantling of apartheid or 'erecting the structures of democracy' as stated in the Nassau Accord.

Members of the ANC Executive sought a number of specific clarifications. For example, the concept could be interpreted as implying that the removal of the military from the townships would itself result in freedom of assembly and discussion. It would be helpful to know what the Group really meant. We clarified that these were separate thoughts: the Government was being asked both to remove the military from the townships and, additonally, to create conditions for freedom of assembly and discussion.

The ANC also wished to know what was meant by the phrase 'power-sharing'. If this were a code word for potential black participation in the racist Tricameral Constitution and its institutions, there would be no basis for a negotiation. We explained that the Government had given an assurance that the agenda would be an open one and that how the balance was struck on the question of power-sharing would be a matter for the negotiations themselves.

On the issue of violence, we clarified that the steps required of the Government would amount to a suspension of the violence of the apartheid system, and it was only in that context that a corresponding suspension of violence by the ANC was being sought. We had made it clear to the Government that it would be unrealistic and impracticable to expect the ANC to renounce violence for all time, regardless of the success or failure of negotiations, nor would we be prepared to endorse any such demand by the Government.

Mr Tambo affirmed the ANC and the Group had a common interest in reaching a point where all could say that apartheid was no more. The ANC appreciated that the concept contained within it the possibility of getting them to that position. He and his colleagues would want about ten days for consultations before giving a firm answer to the Group.

On this encouraging basis we returned to South Africa, having agreed to the possibility of a further round of talks with the ANC in Lusaka in the first week of June in the light of the Government's response.

Sunday, 18 May: Meeting with internal groups

We returned to Johannesburg to consult with the leadership of three internal groups – the UDF, COSATU, and AZAPO. In conveying the main elements of the concept we emphasized that our efforts had been directed to establishing a course in which the black community could enter into negotiations with confidence in an atmosphere devoid of violence. We were not seeking formal reactions from them to the concept but keeping them abreast of the current state of play.

In response, each of these groups responded with keen interest and indicated that prior to adhering to any negotiating process for a solution to South Africa's problems they would need to consult fully with their leadership and affiliates. They undertook to do so.

Monday, 19 May

On the morning of 19 May immediately prior to our meeting with the Cabinet Constitutional Committee in Cape Town, the South African Broadcasting Corporation announced that the South African Defence Forces had successfully carried out raids upon 'ANC bases' in Harare and Gaborone. It was later announced that a similar raid had been made on Lusaka. The Group immediately convened in emergency session. Whilst the reports had not been confirmed, members of the Group expressed shock at the violation of international law and the likely casualties that would result from such action. It was also strongly felt that such wanton action against Commonwealth governments, who were instrumental in setting up the mission on which we were engaged, and especially given its timing, would cast serious doubt on the genuineness of the South African Government's attitude towards a negotiated settlement. Nevertheless, we proceeded to our meeting with the Constitutional Committee as we did not want, in any way, to jeopardize the discussions on our concept whilst there was the slightest chance of making headway. In a subsequent public statement we conveyed sympathy to the Front-Line States concerned and condemned these acts of aggression.

Meeting with the Cabinet Constitutional Committee

The Group met the following members of the Cabinet Constitutional Committee: the Hon. J. C. Heunis, Chairman, (Minister for Constitutional Development and Planning); the Hon. Pik Botha (Minister of Foreign Affairs); the Hon. F. W. de Klerk (Minister of National Education); the Hon. Louis le Grange (Minister of Law and Order); the Hon. G. van N. Viljoen (Minister of Co-operation and Development and Education); the Hon. P. T. C. du Plessis (Minister of Finance); the Hon. S. Botha (Minister of Home Affairs); and the Hon. S. Coetsee (Minister of Justice).

In our presentation to the Committee, we emphasized that the negotiating concept had been with the Government for about nine weeks. Our return to South Africa had been in the belief that the Government wanted to engage in exchanges as a means of advancing the concept. Our most recent meeting with Nelson Mandela had confirmed our view that he was supportive of, and would assist in promoting, the negotiating process. In Lusaka, the ANC had been shown the concept for the first time and had agreed to consult on it. They had, quite reasonably, asked for ten days time to do so before giving a response.

Minister Heunis, as Chairman, reiterated the views of the South African Government. The Group was welcome provided it did not represent outside interference in South Africa's internal affairs. In any negotiating situation there would be many parties, but the South African Government was not just negotiating party; it represented the State, and the institutions of the State would have to endorse any proposals emerging from negotiations. The Government would be guided by the State President's pronouncements on the prerequisites for the process, which he proceeded to enumerate. Central to these was the creation of an atmosphere of non-violence. An essential precondition was, therefore, a renunciation of violence, specifically by the ANC. The phrase 'suspension of violence', used in the first letter of the State President to the Group, had to be interpreted not in the temporary sense, but as a public commitment to reject violence as a means of attaining political goals. The parties at the negotiating table would have to subscribe to such a commitment. Violence was at the moment an impediment to black parties who were willing and ready to join in the negotiating process; the ANC and its partners were responsible for that violence and intimidation. There would have to be a visible reduction in violence before the Government could react to the concept. The Government had proven its commitment to political reforms in South Africa – the onus was on the other side.

We contended that if negotiations were assiduously pursued in good faith and led to positive results, the contemplated 'suspension' of violence would result in the permanent cessation of violence which the Government sought. To ask the ANC or other parties, all of them far weaker than the Government, to renounce violence for all time here and now would be to put them in a position of having to rely absolutely on the Government's intentions and determination to press through the process of negotiation. It was not a question of whether the Group believed in the sincerity of the South African Government, but whether the parties would. It was neither possible nor reasonable to have people forswear the only power available to them should the Government walk away from the negotiating table. For the Government to attribute all violence to the ANC, as it was now doing, was to overlook a situation in which the structures of society, dominated by a relatively small group of people, were founded upon injustice which inevitably led to violence. South Africa was at a crucial turning point in its history. The Government had an obligation to use its power responsibly.

We could not help reflecting that for the average citizen of an established democracy, the proposition that violence should be renounced would appear justified. The position of the blacks in South Africa – deprived of constitutional and political rights, the protection of law, and the means of peaceful protest – is utterly alien to their experience. Based on the totality of all that we saw, there was no question in our own minds that the Government's demand was unrealistic and wholly unreasonable.

It seemed to us that the Government, by reasserting its demand for a one-sided 'renunciation' of violence was reverting to its original position. Nevertheless, we had been informed prior to the meeting that, following it, the Committee of Ministers would consider the issues and make a recommendation to the State President. We felt it imperative to ensure that the South African Government was not left in any doubt that we stood by our concept and that the ball was firmly in its court. We urged the Minister and his colleagues to deliberate again on the concept in the light of our remarks, to make a recommendation to the State President and formally to let us know the South African Government's position. This they agreed to do.

When, later that morning, reports of South African attacks on the capitals of three Commonwealth countries were confirmed, it was our unanimous view that the Government's actions had made our task of bringing the parties to the negotiating table immeasurably more difficult. The ANC announced that the attacks were 'the regime's crystal clear response' to the Commonwealth initiative. They appeared to confirm the worst forebodings of the many organizations and individuals who had warned us not to put faith in the word of the South African Government. It was all too plain that, while talking to the Group about negotiations and peaceful solutions, the Government had been planning these armed attacks.

Later exchanges

On the eve of meeting to prepare our Report we received from the South African Foreign Minister the following letter, dated 29 May 1986, referring to our negotiating concept and the discussions we held with Ministers before leaving South Africa on 19 May 1986:

Dear Mr Fraser and General Obasanjo

I refer to the 'possible negotiating concept' attached to your letter dated 13 March 1986 and the recent discussions you held with Ministers of the South African Government. There are four major questions which are exercising the mind of the South African Government about the possible negotiating concept presented by your Group.

1. The concept of ending or suspending violence.

It is not the choice of a particular word but the concept of terminating violence as a means of achieving political objectives which is relevant. The South African Government cannot accept the suggestion that violence should be discontinued only for as long as negotiations take place. To use violence or the threat of violence as a bargaining counter is unacceptable to the South African Government.

2. Evidence of commitment to a peaceful solution.

The use of violence for political ends cannot be equated with the responsibility of Government to maintain law and order. The South African Government has committed itself to a constitutional dispensation which guarantees

– the removal of racial discrimination;
– sharing of power up to the highest level of government;
– democratic principles including an independent judicial system and the equality of all under the law;
– private property rights;
– private initiative and effective competition;
– fundamental human rights and civil liberties;
– the protection of minority rights in a manner which would ensure that there will be no political domination by any one community of the other;
– freedom of the press and of expression in general;
– freedom of religion and worship;

and is taking substantial steps to carry out this commitment. It would, therefore, be reasonable to expect evidence that the parties presently involved in violence are in principle willing to commit themselves to a peaceful solution through negotiation and in an environment free of violence. A substantial reduction in violence would help to create the atmosphere in which the additional steps could be taken.

3. Intimidation to be abandoned.

It is not only the Government which should permit 'normal political activity' and 'freedom of assembly and discussion'. Other parties need to respect these principles in practice and commit themselves to abandon all forms of intimidation.

4. The nature of the negotiations that are envisaged.

The South African Government is prepared to negotiate with South African citizens about a new constitutional dispensation which will provide for power sharing. It is not interested in negotiation about a transfer of power. The South African Government is committed to a negotiated democratic settlement which addresses the legitimate political aspirations of all South Africans. In contrast, others are on record as wanting a diminished democracy in the form of a one-party state with restricted personal and other freedoms.

The South African Government would welcome further discussions which could accommodate the concerns addressed above.

I would like to thank you and your colleagues for the spirit in which we have been able to conduct our discussions.

Yours sincerely
(Signed) R. F. Botha
Minister of Foreign Affairs

The letter in effect, if not in words, confirmed the South African Government's rejection of the concept of a 'suspension of violence on all sides', both in relation to the concept of 'a suspension' and its relevance to the violence of the apartheid system. It reiterated the notion of a 'constitutional dispensation' unilaterally determined and applied. It was ambivalent on the Government's obligation under the concept to permit 'normal political activity' and 'freedom of assembly and discussion'. But, most significant of all, was its confirmation of the conclusion we record (see 'Conclusions' Chapter) that the Government is not yet ready to negotiate in any genuine way the establishment of a non-racial and representative Government in South Africa.

The letter ended with a statement that the Government would

welcome further discussions which could 'accommodate the concerns' contained in the letter. In the circumstances, we could not but take that to be an invitation to revise our concept to make it more conformable to the Government's notions of dialogue for a new constitutional dispensation. It was therefore an invitation we had to decline. No other course was consistent with our mandate. We therefore replied on 5 June as follows:

My dear Foreign Minister

Thank you for your letter of 29 May 1986 following the discussions between Ministers of the South African Government and the members of the Commonwealth Group in Cape Town on 19 May.

We note that your letter provides a restatement of points which Ministers raised with our Group at the 19 May meeting. Essentially there are two key elements to the points raised by Ministers: that there should be a renunciation of violence and that a de-escalation in the level of violence was necessary before other action might be taken by the Government. The Group explained in some detail its position on these matters and the difficulties which they raised.

Nevertheless, we are convinced that it is possible to achieve negotiations about the democratic future of South Africa if that is the Government's genuine wish, and it is willing to create the circumstances in which co-operation would become possible with the acknowledged leaders of the people of South Africa who would speak and act for negotiation.

We strongly believe that the negotiating concept which we left with the Government is sound and would assist in achieving negotiations in a non-violent atmosphere. This would require acceptance by the South African Government of the spirit and reality of what we have said about violence and a recognition that this applied to all sides. It would also require a deliberate attempt on the part of the South African Government to repair the damage that has been done by its actions of the last few weeks.

We find it difficult to understand how the term suspension of violence provides difficulties for the South African Government particularly as our negotiating concept would involve black leaders arguing in support of the maintenance of peace during the negotiating process. We reiterate that the Lancaster House negotiations continued without the suspension of violence as have many others in situations of conflict.

As to the second point, we reassert that a prior reduction in the level of violence before the Government itself takes specific action in regard to the concept would not be feasible. Acts of aggression were committed against neighbouring countries on the very morning when we discussed the concept with Ministers. This underlines the essential elements of the concept requiring a suspension of violence on all sides and highlights the unreality of asking others to de-escalate violence before action as proposed by the Group is taken by the Government. A suspension of violence or a commitment to non-violence, if in the Government's view the meaning is the same, would obviously in the present context require a commitment to suspend the violence arising from the administration of apartheid. In addition, in the light of recent events, the Government of South Africa would need to give a firm commitment to desist from further aggression against neighbouring states.

In your letter you mentioned two further matters. The first concerned intimidation. In our view the suspension of violence would necessarily involve the end of all intimidation. We emphasize it is only the Government that can establish the circumstances in which normal political activity and freedom of assembly and discussion can take place. This of course is an essential part of our concept.

You then raised questions about the nature of the negotiations. All along we have said that the specific elements of a political settlement are for South Africa to determine. Our charter was never to prescribe the form of the democracy that should evolve in South Africa. That is for South Africans alone. We had noted your assurance that there would be an open agenda at the negotiations against the background of dismantling apartheid and with the objective of the establishment of a just democratic structure.

In the absence both of movement on the part of the Government on the first two major points and a positive response to the concept as a whole, we are unable to see merit in further discussions. This is especially so since actions of recent weeks have made the negotiating climate much more difficult.

Yours sincerely

(Signed) Malcolm Fraser   Olusegun Obasanjo

On 6 June we addressed a letter to all Commonwealth Heads of Government informing them of these developments, drawing their attention to our reply to the South African Government the previous day, and to our 'reluctant but unequivocal judgement that further talks would not lead anywhere in the current circumstances'.

The Nassau Accord asked for the initiation, in the context of a suspension of violence on all sides, a process of dialogue across lines of colour, politics and religion, with a view to establishing a non-racial and representative government.

As we have described, there is no such prospect in view.

Chapter 7
The Regional Dimension

The South African attacks on Harare, Lusaka and Gaborone, early on the morning of Monday, 19 May, Commonwealth capitals we had visited in the course of our work along with others in the region, once more reminded us of the other dimension of the Government's strategy – its determination to force its immediate neighbours to submit to South Africa's economic and political domination of the region. In its dealings with surrounding states, the South African Government has wielded the stick of military and economic sanctions to bend neighbouring nations to its will.

This, the external face of apartheid, is of importance in defending the system and in holding at bay pressure from the international community for ending it.

South Africa's intimidation of its neighbours has rested upon a persistent campaign of destabilization and economic disruption; many of its neighbours have suffered as a result. Military pressure takes many forms. It involves aid (through the supply of materials, training and supporting military action) for dissident movements. It includes action within neighbouring countries, like bombings and other acts of sabotage, as well as independent military action, involving air strikes and commando raids; and sometimes it takes the form of well-planned incursions.

Undoubtedly, Angola and Mozambique have borne the brunt of Pretoria's military aggression, in all its varieties, in the region. Namibia, which should have long ago become a sovereign and independent state, not only remains firmly occupied by South Africa but must mutely witness the use of its territory as a springboard and forward position for Pretoria's military campaigns against surrounding countries, especially Angola.

Several states have entered into 'non-aggression pacts' or security agreements with South Africa in an attempt to stave off further attacks; the Lusaka Accord of February 1984 with Angola and the Nkomati Accord of March 1984 with Mozambique are the best known of these. South Africa violated both these Accords from the very outset, giving the region further proof that it could not be trusted to honour even solemn Treaty obligations.

In March 1984, Mozambique signed the Nkomati Accord with South Africa. Under it, Mozambique undertook to ensure that its territory would not be used for attacks against South Africa while South Africa for its part agreed to terminate forthwith all assistance to the MNR. It has since become abundantly clear that South Africa never intended to honour its commitments. On its own admission, it has continued to support the Mozambique National Resistance (MNR). In the end result, Mozambique's expectations from the Accord have not materialized. The war continues and with it the loss of lives and the mounting destruction of Mozambique's economy.

Lesotho, a country landlocked by South Africa, has suffered two major attacks; the first in December 1983 and the second only last December, besides numerous violations of its territorial integrity. Botswana was attacked in June last year and again in May 1986 along with Zambia and Zimbabwe at a time when we were in South Africa itself in pursuit of a peaceful settlement. We have alluded elsewhere to the implications for our work of these attacks.

But South Africa's punitive power is economic as well as military. Despite protestations to the contrary, South Africa not only believes in the principle of sanctions but has consistently applied them to its neighbours. This economic coercion is largely covert, since the Government likes to pretend to the world that it opposes economic boycotts. Clearly, it has no desire for the international community to follow suit.

Nevertheless, the evidence is clear. The destruction of crucial transport links in Mozambique and Angola by dissident movements receiving support from South Africa has aggravated the dependence of the countries in the region on South Africa's transport network. This gives South Africa enormous power to exercise economic pressure on these countries, which it has not hesitated to use for political ends. For example, in 1980–81 South Africa withdrew locomotives loaned to Zimbabwe. From time to time Botswana has experienced delays in securing railway wagons vital for its beef exports. Zimbabwe, for example, has had to incur heavy costs by stationing troops to guard a vital transport corridor through Mozambique.

Beginning in the mid-1970s but especially since 1980, South Africa has sought to disrupt and destroy the alternative transport networks and port opportunities opened to the landlocked countries of the region with the independence of Angola and Mozambique and the formation of the Southern African Development Co-ordination Conference (SADCC). The aim has been to drive regional trade through the more expensive transportation routes of South Africa.

Other economic pressures have included the destruction of power lines and oil installations, ratcheting up the cost of fuel and transport; the destruction of houses, schools, factories and equipment; and the exploitation of those countries which act as exporters of cheap labour to South African mines, industry and agriculture. For example, the remittances of migrant workers have come to be a major source of revenue for the Government of Mozambique, and this link has been manipulated by the South Africans to cause considerable economic dislocation. South Africa has reduced Mozambican migrant workers by some 60 per cent since independence, and has terminated the preferential gold agreement under which a portion of the wages of migrant workers was remitted to the Government in gold at a fixed rate.

Botswana, Lesotho, and Swaziland are worst placed to escape from dependence on South Africa. Such is the degree of their dependence on the South African economy that only sheer political will has enabled them to avoid full absorption into the apartheid economy. Here too the regime has exploited the vulnerability of these countries in furtherance of its regional objective.

The cost of South Africa's 'total strategy', in terms of human life, is incalculable, although some estimate the loss of life at 100,000, and those made homeless at one million. But the grave impact of these destabilization policies on SADCC economies – through lower revenues from exports, tourism and transport; from lower output and reduced capacity; from the waste of social and economic investment and the increasing diversion of resources into defence – can be calculated. The total cost to those nine countries is estimated at over US$10 billion in the period 1980–1984. That huge sum far exceeds the total foreign assistance received by SADCC, and is equivalent to about one third of all Member States' export earnings during that period. Some argue that this growing burden may well be of the order of US$4 or 5 billion a year for the SADCC region as a whole.

It is the reality of this dependence which led Botswana's Vice-President Peter Mmusi to observe in January that 'The abolition of apartheid could be the greatest single contribution which could be made to the economic development of the region.' This is the reason why countries whose economies are intertwined with that of South Africa, and who inevitably remain vulnerable, none the less regard the imposition of economic sanctions on South Africa as the sole remaining instrument for effective change in the absence of serious negotiations by the South African Government with genuine black leaders.

Front-Line leaders have repeatedly called on the international community to take just that course; and they have done so in the conviction that, in the prevailing circumstances, it is the only peaceful resort which will shorten the agony unleashed on the region by apartheid over so many decades.

Nobody who cares for the future of a free and non-racial South Africa, rich in resources and productive in its trade and commerce, would wish to see the destruction of its economic and industrial base. Yet that will be the consequence if the continuing failure to dismantle apartheid and peacefully negotiate a political settlement is allowed to run in parallel with an external policy of conflict and destruction, involving the whole sub-continent.

Apartheid South Africa poses a wide threat well beyond its borders.

Chapter Eight
Conclusions

Our work in South Africa has been a moving personal experience for every one of us. We arrived in the country when there was carnage in Alexandra. On the day of our final departure from Cape Town, Crossroads was on fire and a pall of smoke hung in the sky. We saw a country in upheaval and witnessed great human suffering. Even as we write, the killings continue.

Each of us pondered at length the invitation to serve on the Group. It was clear that our task would be immensely difficult. Its success would depend, ultimately, on the good faith of the South African Government and on the co-operation of all significant sections of South African society. It was only because we were persuaded that, whatever the odds, this was a task worth attempting that we accepted. In the course of our successive visits to South Africa, and on becoming better acquainted with the effects of apartheid and the scale of the country's antagonisms, there could be little doubt that the alternative to a negotiated solution would be appalling chaos, bloodshed and destruction. We are concerned that the South African Government's rejection, in effect, of our negotiating concept compounded by its armed aggression against Botswana, Zambia and Zimbabwe makes those dangers more imminent and the prospect of negotiations more difficult.

With members from diverse national and political backgrounds, we possessed particular advantages. We believe we acquired the confidence and trust of all the principal black leaders and organizations within the country, as well as the liberation movements outside. We were able to travel freely throughout South Africa, to visit black townships normally not accessible to outsiders and to talk to a diverse spectrum of opin-

Ted Scott makes a friend in Alexandra township, Johannesburg. (Photo: Malcolm Fraser)

ion including opposition parties, trade unions, church leaders, businessmen, women's groups and civil rights activists. In extensive discussions with the State President and many of his Ministers, we also gained valuable insights into the Government's own thinking and future plans. The range of contacts we made, enabling us to understand the complexities of the situation, was probably unique; the frankness and the openness of the discussions unlikely to be replicated in the near future. We, therefore, permit ourselves some broader reflections.

Our mandate was to foster a process of negotiation across lines of colour, politics and religion, with a view to establishing a non-racial and representative government. It is our considered view that, despite appearances and statements to the contrary, the South African Government is not yet ready to negotiate such a future – except on its own terms. Those terms, both in regard to objectives and modalities, fall far short of reasonable black expectations and well accepted democratic norms and principles.

The objectives of any negotiations, as Commonwealth leaders

agreed at Nassau, and as all the non-white people of South Africa as well as increasing numbers of whites demand, would be the dismantling of the apartheid system and the erection of the structures of democracy in South Africa. We rejected as impractical the suggestion that the whole complex web of apartheid legislation be repealed as a prelude to negotiation; we were concerned to ensure, however, that there should be a firm and unambiguous commitment by the Government to ending apartheid in order to provide integrity to the negotiating agenda and the negotiating process – as well as specific and meaningful steps taken to that end. It needs to be remembered that apartheid goes beyond institutionalized racial discrimination and economic exploitation; it is primarily a means of keeping ultimate political and economic power in the hands of the white minority. Any reservations by the Government about dismantling apartheid would inevitably and understandably be viewed by the vast majority as a ploy for perpetuating white power in a new guise, a willingness to change its form but not abandon its substance.

The Government told us categorically that it was prepared to contemplate negotiations with a completely open agenda, where everything would be on the table. However, as we have pointed out elsewhere, in some respects, the open agenda appeared to be circumscribed. Nevertheless, for the purposes of our discussions we gave the South African Government the benefit of the doubt in our minds. In the Government's thinking, there were a number of non-negotiables; for example, the concept of group rights – the very basis of the apartheid system – was sacrosanct; the 'homelands' created in furtherance of that concept would not disappear, but be reinforced with the emergence of an 'independent' KwaNdebele; the principle of one man one vote in a unitary state was beyond the realm of possibility; the Population Registration Act would continue; and the present Tricameral Constitution which institutionalises racism must be the vehicle for future constitutional reform.

From these and other recent developments, we draw the conclusion that while the Government claims to be ready to negotiate, it is in truth not yet prepared to negotiate fundamental change, nor to countenance the creation of genuine democratic structures, nor to face the prospect of the end of white domination and white power in the foreseeable future. Its programme of reform does not end apartheid, but seeks to give it a less inhuman face. Its quest is power-sharing, but without surrendering overall white control.

In regard to the modalities of negotiation, the Government's position has a considerable element of wishful thinking. The Government is willing and ready to negotiate with 'responsible' leaders; if only violence and 'intimidation' would abate, these leaders would be ready to come to the negotiating table to strike a deal. Although we were never told by the Government who these 'responsible' leaders might be – indeed, the Government assured us it would not prescribe or limit the people's choice – it could be inferred that prominent among them would be the 'homelands' leaders whom the Government repeatedly urged us to see. With the exception of Chief Buthelezi, the 'homeland' leaders have no real political standing or following and would not, in our view, be credible parties in a negotiation to resolve South Africa's deepening crisis. It is not for us to prescribe or advise who the parties to a genuine negotiation might be; but we noted as significant the Government's allergy to our proposal that they should be the 'true', 'authentic' or 'acknowledged' leaders of the people.

Negotiations leading to fundamental political change and the erection of democratic structures will only be possible if the South African Government is prepared to deal with leaders of the people's choosing rather than with puppets of its own creation. President Botha's recent statements expressing his determination to 'break' the ANC bode ill for the country's future. There can be no negotiated settlement in South Africa without the ANC; the breadth of its support is incontestable; and this support is growing. Among the many striking figures whom we met in the course of our work, Nelson Mandela and Oliver Tambo stand out. Their reasonableness, absence of rancour and readiness to find negotiated solutions which, while creating genuine democratic structures would still give the whites a feeling of security and participation, impressed us

A typical black township welcome for the EPG. (Photo: Moni Malhoutra)

Moutse Chiefs and residents provide tea for the Group after telling of pressure to submit to their incorporation into the 'homeland' of KwaNdebele. (Photo: Malcolm Fraser)

deeply. If the Government finds itself unable to talk with men like Mandela and Tambo, then the future of South Africa is bleak indeed.

The Government made it clear that it did not regard the ANC as the only other party to negotiations. We agree, but would emphasize that the ANC is a necessary party. The Government itself acknowledges this, if only by blaming the ANC for most of the violence. The open identification with the ANC through banners and songs, in funerals and in churches throughout the country, despite the risks involved, supports the widely-held belief that if an election were held today on the basis of universal franchise the ANC would win it. Whatever the truth of that assertion, we none the less recognize that black political opinion is not monolithic. If, therefore, the Government is serious about negotiations, it must create conditions in which free political activity becomes possible, and political parties and leaders are able to function effectively and test the extent of their popular support. Tragically, the whole thrust of Government policy has been to thwart such legitimate leadership from emerging and destroy it where it does. Even non-violent organizations like the UDF have been subjected to harassment and persecution.

Behind these attitudes lurks a deeper truth. After more than 18 months of persistent unrest, upheaval, and killings unprecedented in the country's history, the Government believes that it can contain the situation indefinitely by use of force. We were repeatedly told by Ministers that the Government had deployed only a fraction of the power at its disposal. Although the Government's confidence may be valid in the short term, but at great human cost, it is plainly misplaced in the longer term. South Africa is predominantly a country of black people. To believe that they can be indefinitely suppressed is an act of self-delusion.

By pandering to right-wing anxieties and demands, the Government fortifies them, compounding its own problems and losing whatever initiative it may have possessed. It is also in danger of falling between two stools. Its promises of reform have created anxiety among certain sections of its supporters and contributed to a growing white backlash; yet the reforms themselves have made little impact on black attitudes or aspirations – save to confirm the Government's implacable resistance to significant change.

While right-wing opposition cannot be ignored, it would be fatal to give it a veto. Indeed, we gained the impression that white opinion as a whole may be ahead of the Government in significant respects, ready to respond positively if given a bold lead.

We are left with the impression of a divided Government. Yet even the more enlightened Ministers whom we met seem to be out of touch with the mood in the black townships, the rising tide of anger and impatience within them, and the extent of black mobilization. And so, of course, are the great generality of white South Africans – only some ten per cent of whom, we were told, have ever seen conditions in a township.

Put in the most simple way, the blacks have had enough of apartheid. They are no longer prepared to submit to its oppression, discrimination and exploitation. They can no longer stomach being treated as aliens in their own country. They have confidence not merely in the justice of their cause, but in the inevitability of their victory. Unlike the earlier periods of unrest and Government attempts to stamp out protest, there has been during the last 18 months no outflow of black refugees from South Africa. The strength of black convictions is now matched by a readiness to die for those convictions. They will, therefore, sustain their struggle, whatever the cost.

The campaign against collaborators, and the ruthless elimination of agents of white authority, will continue. More and more black townships will be rendered ungovernable, and the process of creating popular structures of self-government within them will gather momentum. The number of street and area committees will increase and their functions will progressively enlarge.

The writ of the Government will be increasingly circumscribed. Inter-black rivalry and violence, partly encouraged and fomented by the Government, will grow, making the task of negotiating a settlement even more difficult. Political upheaval and social unrest will accelerate the flight of capital and professional skills and the economy's downward spiral.

Amidst all this gloom the quality of the country's black leaders shines through. Their achievement in bringing about popular and trade union mobilization in the face of huge odds commands respect. Their idealism, their genuine sense of non-racialism, and their readiness not only to forget but to forgive, compel admiration. These are precious assets which a new South Africa will need; they may be lost altogether if the Government continues to shrink from taking the necessary political decisions with a sense of urgency. The options are diminishing by the day.

The Government faces difficult choices. Its obduracy and intransigence wrecked the Commonwealth's initiative, but the issues themselves will not go away, nor can they be bombed out of existence. It is not sanctions which will destroy the country but the persistence of apartheid and the Government's failure to engage in fundamental political reform.

In our Report we have addressed in turn the five steps which the Nassau Accord called on the authorities in Pretoria to take 'in a genuine manner and as a matter of urgency'. They, and our conclusions with regard to them, are as follows:

● **Declare that the system of apartheid will be dismantled and specific and meaningful action taken in fulfilment of that intent.**

We have examined the Government's 'programme of reform' and have been forced to conclude that at present there is no genuine intention on the part of the South African Government to dismantle apartheid.

● **Terminate the existing state of emergency.**

Although the state of emergency was technically lifted, the substantive powers remain broadly in force under the ordinary laws of the land which, even now, are being further strengthened in this direction.

● **Release immediately and unconditionally Nelson**

Mandela and all others imprisoned and detained for their opposition to apartheid.

Nelson Mandela and other political leaders remain in prison.

● **Establish political freedom and specifically lift the existing ban on the African National Congress and other political parties.**

Political freedom is far from being established; if anything, it is being more rigorously curtailed. The ANC and other political parties remain banned.

● **Initiate, in the context of a suspension of violence on all sides, a process of dialogue across lines of colour, politics and religion, with a view to establishing a nonracial and representative government.**

The cycle of violence and counter-violence has spiralled and there is no present prospect of a process of dialogue leading to the establishment of a non-racial and representative government.

Overall, the concrete and adequate progress looked for in the Nassau Accord towards the objectives of 'dismantling apartheid and erecting the structures of democracy in South Africa' has not materialized.

Indeed, in recent weeks the Government would appear to have moved consciously away from any realistic negotiating process. It is not just their communications with us which have indicated a hardening of attitude. The same message has been clear in the State President's speech in May, the bombing of three neighbouring Commonwealth countries even while we were in discussion with senior Ministers, the denigration and smearing of the ANC, the retreat from the earlier readiness to accept 'suspension' as opposed to 'renunciation' of violence, the seeking of greater security powers for the police and military on top of the massive powers they already have, the renewed determination to suppress public meetings and free speech and to harass black leaders, and not least the more recent raids on Angolan ports.

For all the people of South Africa and of the sub-region as a whole, the certain prospect is of an even sharper decline into

Group at work in Marlborough House, venue of their London meetings. From right: General Obasanjo, Lord Barber, Swaran Singh, Ted Scott, Nita Barrow; Neville Linton and Stuart Mole (Commonwealth Secretariat, standing). (Photo: Hugh Craft)

violence and bloodshed with all its attendant human costs. A racial conflagration with frightening implications threatens. The unco-ordinated violence of today could become in the not too distant future a major armed conflict spilling well beyond South Africa's borders. In such circumstances the entire economic fabric of the country would indeed be destroyed. Up to now those responsible for the armed resistance in South Africa have shown great regard for innocent lives. Unless the cycle of violence is broken, full-fledged guerrilla warfare as practised in other parts of the world, in which 'soft' civilian targets become prime targets in a reign of terror and counter-terror, may come to pass. In the absence of significant moves to break the cycle of violence we see the prospect as inevitable and that in the very foreseeable future.

What can be done? What remaining influence does the international community have? What can major states do to help avert an otherwise inevitable disaster? There may be no course available that can guarantee a significantly more peaceful solution. But against the background in which ever-increasing violence will be a certainty, the question of further measures immediately springs to mind. As the Nassau Accord makes clear, Commonwealth Heads of Government have agreed that, in the event of adequate progress not having been made in South Africa within a period of six months, they would consider further measures.

While we are not determining the nature or extent of any measures which might be adopted, or their effectiveness, we point to the fact that the Government of South Africa has itself used economic measures against its neighbours and that such measures are patently instruments of its own national policy. We are convinced that the South African Government is concerned about the adoption of effective economic measures against it. If it comes to the conclusion that it would always remain protected from such measures, the process of change in South Africa is unlikely to increase in momentum and the descent into violence would be accelerated. In these circumstances, the cost in lives may have to be counted in millions.

From the point of view of the black leadership, the course now taken by the world community will have the greatest significance. That leadership has already come to the view that diplomatic persuasion has not and will not move the South African Government sufficiently. If it also comes to believe that the world community will never exercise sufficient effective pressure through other measures in support of their cause, they will have only one option remaining: that of ever-increasing violence. Once decisions involving greater violence are made on both sides, they carry an inevitability of their own and are difficult, if not impossible, to reverse, except as a result of exhaustion through prolonged conflict.

The question in front of Heads of Government is in our view clear. It is not whether such measures will compel change; it is already the case that their absence and Pretoria's belief that they need not be feared, defers change. Is the Commonwealth to stand by and allow the cycle of violence to spiral? Or will it take concerted action of an effective kind? Such action may offer the last opportunity to avert what could be the worst bloodbath since the Second World War.

We hope that this Report will assist the Commonwealth – and the wider international community – in helping all the people of South Africa save themselves from that awesome tragedy.

Annex 1

The Commonwealth Accord on Southern Africa

1. We consider that South Africa's continuing refusal to dismantle apartheid, its illegal occupation of Namibia, and its aggression against its neighbours constitute a serious challenge to the values and principles of the Commonwealth, a challenge which Commonwealth countries cannot ignore. At New Delhi we expressed the view that 'only the eradication of apartheid and the establishment of majority rule on the basis of free and fair exercise of universal adult suffrage by all the people in a united and non-fragmented South Africa can lead to a just and lasting solution of the explosive situation prevailing in Southern Africa'. We are united in the belief that reliance on the range of pressures adopted so far has not resulted in the fundamental changes we have sought over many years. The growing crisis and intensified repression in South Africa mean that apartheid must be dismantled now if a greater tragedy is to be averted and that concerted pressure must be brought to bear to achieve that end. We consider that the situation calls for urgent practical steps.

2. We, therefore, call on the authorities in Pretoria for the following steps to be taken in a genuine manner and as a matter of urgency:

 (a) Declare that the system of apartheid will be dismantled and specific and meaningful action taken in fulfilment of that intent.

 (b) Terminate the existing state of emergency.

 (c) Release immediately and unconditionally Nelson Mandela and all others imprisoned and detained for their opposition to apartheid.

 (d) Establish political freedom and specifically lift the existing ban on the African National Congress and other political parties.

 (e) Initiate, in the context of a suspension of violence on all sides, a process of dialogue across lines of colour, politics and religion, with a view to establishing a non-racial and representative government.

3. We have agreed on a number of measures which have as their rationale impressing on the authorities in Pretoria the compelling urgency of dismantling apartheid and erecting the structures of democracy in South

Africa. The latter, in particular, demands a process of dialogue involving the true representatives of the majority black population of South Africa. We believe that we must do all we can to assist that process, while recognizing that the forms of political settlement in South Africa are for the people of that country – all the people – to determine.

4. To this end, we have decided to establish a small group of eminent Commonwealth persons to encourage through all practicable ways the evolution of that necessary process of political dialogue. We are not unmindful of the difficulties such an effort will encounter, including the possibility of initial rejection by the South African authorities, but we believe it to be our duty to leave nothing undone that might contribute to peaceful change in South Africa and avoid the dreadful prospect of violent conflict that looms over South Africa, threatening people of all races in the country, and the peace and stability of the entire Southern Africa region.

5. We are asking the President of Zambia and the Prime Ministers of Australia, The Bahamas, Canada, India, the United Kingdom and Zimbabwe to develop with the Secretary-General the modalities of this effort to assist the process of political dialogue in South Africa. We would look to the group of eminent persons to seek to facilitate the processes of dialogue referred to in paragraph 2(e) above and by all practicable means to advance the fulfilment of the objectives of this Accord.

6. For our part, we have as an earnest of our opposition to apartheid reached accord on a programme of common action as follows:

   (i) We declare the Commonwealth's support for the strictest enforcement of the mandatory arms embargo against South Africa, in accordance with United Nations Security Council Resolutions 418 and 558, and commit ourselves to prosecute violators to the fullest extent of the law;

  (ii) we reaffirm the Gleneagles Declaration of 1977, which called upon Commonwealth members to take every practical step to discourage sporting contacts with South Africa;

 (iii) we agree upon, and commend to other governments, the adoption of the following further economic measures against South Africa, which have already been adopted by a number of member countries:

    (a) a ban on all new government loans to the Government of South Africa and its agencies;

(b) a readiness to take unilaterally what action may be possible to preclude the import of Krugerrands;

(c) no Government funding for trade missions to South Africa or for participation in exhibitions and trade fairs in South Africa;

(d) a ban on the sale and export of computer equipment capable of use by South African military forces, police or security forces;

(e) a ban on new contracts for the sale and export of nuclear goods, materials and technology to South Africa;

(f) a ban on the sale and export of oil to South Africa;

(g) a strict and rigorously controlled embargo on imports of arms, ammunition, military vehicles and paramilitary equipment from South Africa;

(h) an embargo on all military co-operation with South Africa; and

(i) discouragement of all cultural and scientific events except where these contribute towards the ending of apartheid or have no possible role in promoting it.

7. It is our hope that the process and measures we have agreed upon will help to bring about concrete progress towards the objectives stated above in six months. The Heads of Government mentioned in paragraph 5 above, or their representatives, will then meet to review the situation. If in their opinion adequate progress has not been made within this period, we agree to consider the adoption of further measures. Some of us would, in that event, consider the following steps among others:

(a) a ban on air links with South Africa;

(b) a ban on new investment or reinvestment of profits earned in South Africa;

(c) a ban on the import of agricultural products from South Africa;

(d) the termination of double taxation agreements with South Africa;

(e) the termination of all government assistance to investment in, and trade with, South Africa;

(f) a ban on all government procurement in South Africa;

(g) a ban on government contracts with majority-owned South African companies;

(h) a ban on the promotion of tourism to South Africa.

8. Finally, we agree that should all of the above measures fail to produce the desired results within a reasonable period, further effective measures will have to be considered. Many of us have either taken or are prepared to take measures which go beyond those listed above, and each of us will pursue the objectives of this Accord in all the ways and through all appropriate fora open to us. We believe, however, that in pursuing this programme jointly, we enlarge the prospects of an orderly transition to social, economic and political justice in South Africa and peace and stability in the Southern Africa region as a whole.

Lyford Cay, Nassau
20 October 1985

Letter Dated 13 December 1985 from the Co-Chairmen to the State President of South Africa and the State President's Reply of 24 December 1985

> Marlborough House
> Pall Mall
> London SW1Y 5HX
> 13 December 1985

Dear Mr State President,

We are writing on behalf of the seven-member Group established by Commonwealth Heads of Government pursuant to their Nassau 'Accord on Southern Africa'. You may recall that the text of the Accord together with the composition of our Group was transmitted at the request of the Commonwealth Secretary-General to your Government on 25 November by the diplomatic representatives of Australia, Britain and Canada. The Accord constitutes the broad mandate under which we are working.

We have today concluded our first meeting in London. We are anxious to get down to business as quickly as possible in a spirit of helpfulness and with the co-operation of all the parties concerned, working quietly and essentially in non-public ways. We therefore attach the utmost importance to visiting South Africa for consultations with your Government and all who are in a position to contribute to the achievement of our objective. This we perceive as being essential for encouraging and facilitating the process of political dialogue envisaged in the Accord.

Consistent with our purpose, we would need while in South Africa to meet with the Government, with the true representatives of the black population as well as with others whose views would be relevant to such a process. In our discussions we will seek to clarify attitudes towards beginning the dialogue envisaged and to elicit views on ways of advancing it.

We have noted with appreciation the statement by your Foreign Minister, The Hon. Pik Botha, on 26 November. Since it is our clear wish that our first contacts should if possible be with your Government, we would very much hope that a visit along the lines outlined above could be arranged at the earliest possible date, preferably before the end of January, 1986.

Yours sincerely,

Malcolm Fraser   Olusegun Obasanjo
Co-Chairman   Co-Chairman

HE Mr P. W. Botha,
State President,
Republic of South Africa

Union Buildings
Pretoria
24 December 1985

Gentlemen

I acknowledge your letter of 13 December 1985 as conveyed to the Department of Foreign Affairs by the Ambassadors of Canada, United Kingdom and Australia on 16 December 1985.

I am encouraged by your positive reaction to the statement issued by my Minister of Foreign Affairs on 26 November 1985 setting out the South African Government's attitude with regard to the Commonwealth initiative.

I am prepared to approach this initiative constructively. I hope that you will be equally constructive in your approach. The Commonwealth Group can do incalculable harm if it sees itself as a pressure group charged with the task of extracting concessions from the Government and generally engaged in prescribing solutions to problems which are the sole concern of South Africans.

If, on the other hand, it wants to be informed of the situation in South Africa and confines itself to promoting peaceful political dialogue and, moreover, can be seen to be unbiased in this respect, it could serve a useful purpose. I agree that a suspension of violence is a requirement for dialogue. I would hope, therefore, that the Commonwealth Group will discourage violence and avoid action or comment which might be seen or interpreted as encouragement to those promoting or supporting violence.

To ensure that there is no misunderstanding concerning the policies and objectives of my Government, let me state that we are determined to proceed with our reform programme which has already reached an advanced stage, whatever the obstacles we have to contend with; and we want to get moving with the negotiations. The sooner this can be done the better, for this is the key to the solution of our problems. Our political programme provides for power sharing, subject only to the protection of the rights of all minorities, and we are reconciled to the eventual disappearance of white domination. All our communities must have a fair say in Government and this is what we shall be striving to achieve in the course of the negotiations. It presages the end of racial discrimination. But we need the co-operation of all our communities in constructing an alternative system of Government for South Africa. I trust that the Group will ensure that it does nothing which might impede the creation of a climate conducive to such co-operation.

You are welcome to visit South Africa and to consult with my Government and the representatives of the various population groups on the basis of the foregoing considerations. The modalities and timing can be arranged to our mutual satisfaction at functional level in the course of January 1986.

Yours sincerely

P. W. BOTHA
STATE PRESIDENT OF THE
REPUBLIC OF SOUTH AFRICA

Mr Malcolm Fraser
General Olusegun Obasanjo
Co-Chairmen
Commonwealth Eminent Persons Group
LONDON

Annex 3

The Group's Programme of Visits and Meetings

The following statement lists the meetings we had in the course of our work. Not listed are many of the people with whom we met both formally and informally within and outside South Africa. There were others whom we were unable to meet by reason of their absence from South Africa or unavoidable commitments elsewhere; and there were a few who declined our approaches.

Our work generated much interest in South Africa and beyond, and we received a steady flow of petitions and communications. To the many individuals and groups, too numerous to mention here by name, who made their views known to us we express our gratitude.

We owe a special debt to the three Commonwealth Ambassadors in South Africa – Australia, Britain and Canada – and members of their Missions, for their advice and practical assistance in facilitating our work in South Africa. Our thanks are also due to the South African Department of Foreign Affairs for the assistance and courtesies extended to us.

Formal Meetings of the Group

The Group convened in formal session on five occasions at Marlborough House, the Commonwealth Secretariat Headquarters in London, as follows:

- – 12–13 December 1985
- – 23 January 1986 (Co-Chairmen)
- – 13–14 February 1986
- – 30 April–1 May 1986
- – 4–7 June 1986

At these meetings the Group undertook consultations with senior officials of the South African Government on several occasions; and benefited from the submissions of numerous experts on South African affairs.

Preliminary Visit to South Africa (Undertaken By Mr Malcolm Fraser and General Olusegun Obasanjo, the Co-Chairmen, and Dame Nita Barrow)

Sunday, 16 February – Cape Town

- Ambassadors of Australia, Britain and Canada

Monday, 17 February – Cape Town

- The Hon. J. C. Heunis, Minister for Constitutional Development and Planning
- Dr Alex Boraine, former Progressive Federal Party (PFP)
- The Hon. R. F. (Pik) Botha, Minister of Foreign Affairs
- General The Hon. Magnus A. Malan, Minister of Defence
- Dr Allan Boesak, Patron of the United Democratic Front (UDF) and President of the World Alliance of Reformed Churches

Tuesday, 18 February – Cape Town

- Mr Colin Eglin, MP, Leader of the PFP
- The UDF Western Cape Executive
- The Hon. Louis le Grange, Minister of Law and Order
- The Hon. S. Coetsee, Minister of Justice

Wednesday, 19 February – Johannesburg

- Bishop Desmond Tutu, Anglican Bishop of Johannesburg
- The South African Council of Churches (SACC)
- Mrs Winnie Mandela
- A delegation from Alexandra township
- An invited group of leading South African businessmen

Thursday, 20 February – Johannesburg

- Visit to Soweto
- Soweto Civic Association
- UDF Executive, Transvaal and Natal Regions
- Congress of South African Trade Unions (COSATU)
- Black Sash
- The Azanian People's Organization (AZAPO)

Friday, 21 February – Johannesburg and Cape Town

- The General Secretary, the General and Allied Workers' Union (GAWU)*

---

* The Group sometimes divided to undertake different assignments, in sub-groups or individually. These assignments are indicated by a single asterisk for the remainder of Annex III.

- Visit to Alexandra township*
- The Hon. J. C. Heunis, Minister of Constitutional Development and Planning*
- Mr Nelson Mandela at Pollsmoor Prison (permission granted to General Obasanjo alone)
- A Conservative Party representative*
- The Hon. R. F. (Pik) Botha, Minister of Foreign Affairs

Saturday, 22 February – Port Elizabeth

- Dr Allan Boesak
- UDF members, Port Elizabeth
- Drive to Walmer township

Visit to Neighbouring States

Sunday, 23 February – Maseru, Lesotho

- HM King Moshoeshoe II
- Military Council and members of the Council of Ministers

Monday, 24 February – Maseru, Lesotho and Gaborone, Botswana

- HM King Moshoeshoe II
- HE Dr Quett K. J. Masire, President of Botswana

Tuesday, 25 February – Gaborone, Botswana and Harare, Zimbabwe

- The Hon. P. S. Mmusi, Vice-President of Botswana
- The Hon. Robert Mugabe, Prime Minister of Zimbabwe
- Mr Dennis Norman, former Minister of Agriculture, Zimbabwe

Thursday, 27 February – Lusaka, Zambia

- HE Dr Kenneth Kaunda, President of Zambia

Friday, 28 February – Lusaka, Zambia

- President Oliver Tambo and other members of the Executive of the African National Congress (ANC)
- HE Dr Kenneth Kaunda, President of Zambia

Saturday, 1 March – Luanda, Angola

- HE José Eduardo dos Santos, President of the People's Republic of Angola

First Visit of the Full Group to South Africa

Sunday, 2 March – Cape Town

- Ambassadors of Australia, Britain and Canada

Monday, 3 March – Cape Town

- The Hon. J. C. Heunis, Minister for Constitutional Development and Planning
- The Hon. B. J. du Plessis, Minister of Finance
- The Hon. R. F. (Pik) Botha, Minister of Foreign Affairs
- Mr Anthony Heard, Editor, the *Cape Times*
- An invited group of Cape Town academics

Tuesday, 4 March – Cape Town

- Mr Colin Eglin, MP, Leader of the PFP and Mrs Helen Suzman, MP
- Dr Allan Boesak
- Crossroads township representatives; followed by visit to Crossroads township
- The Hon. Dr Gerrit Viljoen, Minister of Co-operation, Development and Education

Wednesday, 5 March – Port Elizabeth* and the Midlands region*

- Visit to black townships of New Brighton and Soweto (Port Elizabeth)
- UDF Eastern Cape Executive and Port Elizabeth Black Community Organizations (PEBCO)
- Visit to De Aar, Hanover, Middelburg, Graaff-Reinet and Cradock in the Midlands region*

Thursday, 6 March – Johannesburg and Pretoria

- Executive Members of the South African Council of Churches (SACC)
- Father Smangaliso Mkhatshwa, Secretary-General, South African Catholic Bishops Conference (SACBC)
- National Executive of the Dutch Reformed Church (NGK)
- Visit to Atteridgeville and Mamelodi townships*
- Visit to Alexandra and Tembisa townships*
- Invited group of leading businessmen

Friday, 7 March – Johannesburg

- Mrs Winnie Mandela
- An invited group of Johannesburg academics
- Representatives of 'Women Under Apartheid' Organization
- Federated Chambers of Industry (FCI) and the National Federation of Chambers of Commerce (NAFCOC)
- Black Sash
- Members of AZAPO National Executive

Saturday, 8 March – Johannesburg

- Dr and Mrs Max Coleman, Detainees' Parents' Support Committee
- Visit to Moutse District and Motatama, Krugersdorp and Groblersdal*

Sunday, 9 March – Johannesburg

- Member of the National Executive of the UDF

Monday, 10 March – Johannesburg and Durban

- Association of Chambers of Commerce (ASSOCOM)
- Mr T. M. Molatlhwa, 'Foreign Minister' and Mr S. L. L. Rathebe 'Manpower Minister' of Bophuthatswana
- The Hon. Reverend Allan Hendrickse, Minister without Portfolio and Chairman of the House of Representatives; Chief Mangosuthu Buthelezi, Chief Minister of KwaZulu and President of Inkatha; and Chief Enos Mabuza, Chief Minister of KwaNgwane, jointly
- Chief Mangosuthu Buthelezi
- Archbishop Hurley, Chairman, SACBC (in Durban)
- Leading non-governmental personalities (in Durban)

Tuesday, 11 March – Durban, Port Elizabeth and Cape Town

- Representatives of Natal Indian Congress
- Visit to Phoenix settlement and KwaMashu
- Mr Frank Martin, Member of the Natal Executive Committee*
- Ecumenical Service conducted by Dr Allan Boesak (in Port Elizabeth)

Wednesday, 12 March – Cape Town

- The Hon. F. W. de Klerk, Minister of Home Affairs and National Education
- The Hon. Amichand Rajbansi, Minister without Portfolio and Chairman, House of Delegates*
- The Hon. R. F. (Pik) Botha, Minister of Foreign Affairs

- Mr Nelson Mandela at Pollsmoor Prison
- HE Mr P. W. Botha, State President of the Republic of South Africa
- The Hon. S. Coetsee, Minister of Justice
- The Hon. J. C. Heunis, Minister for Constitutional Development and Planning

Thursday, 13 March – Cape Town

- Members of the UDF National Executive
- Ambassadors of Australia, Britain and Canada

Visit by General Obasanjo and Mr Malecela to Front-line States and Nigeria

Tuesday, 1 April – Lagos, Nigeria

- HE Major-General I. B. Babangida, President and Commander-in-Chief of the Federal Republic of Nigeria*

Thursday, 3 April – Harare, Zimbabwe and Lusaka, Zambia

- The Hon. Robert Mugabe, Prime Minister of Zimbabwe
- HE Dr Kenneth Kaunda, President of Zambia
- President Oliver Tambo and members of the ANC Executive

Meeting of the Group in London

Wednesday, 30 April

- Mr Johnson Mlambo, Chairman and members of the Executive of Pan-Africanist Congress of Azania (PAC)

Second Visit by the Group to South Africa and Zambia

Thursday, 13 May – Cape Town

- Ambassadors of Australia, Britain and Canada
- The Hon. R. F. (Pik) Botha, Minister of Foreign Affairs, later joined by the Hon. B. J. du Plessis, Minister of Finance and the Hon. Stoffel Botha, Minister of Home Affairs

- Dr Allan Boesak
- Group of residents from Hout Bay★
- The Hon. S. Coetsee, Minister of Justice

Friday, 16 May – Cape Town and Lusaka

- Mr Nelson Mandela at Pollsmoor Prison
- The Hon. R. F. (Pik) Botha, Minister of Foreign Affairs
- HE Dr Kenneth Kaunda, President of Zambia

Saturday, 17 May – Lusaka, Zambia

- HE Dr Kenneth Kaunda, President of Zambia★
- President Oliver Tambo and other members of the Executive of the ANC

Sunday, 18 May – Johannesburg

- Executive of COSATU
- Members of AZAPO National Executive
- Members of UDF National Executive

Monday, 19 May – Cape Town

- The Cabinet Constitutional Committee:
  The Hon. J. C. Heunis (Chairman), Minister for Constitutional Development and Planning; The Hon. R. F. (Pik) Botha, Minister of Foreign Affairs; The Hon. F. W. de Klerk, Minister of National Education; The Hon. Louis le Grange, Minister of Law and Order; The Hon. Dr Gerrit Viljoen, Minister for Co-operation, Development and Education; The Hon. B. J. du Plessis, Minister of Finance; The Hon. S. Botha, Minister of Home Affairs and the Hon. S. Coetsee, Minister of Justice
- Mrs Winnie Mandela

Other Visits and Meetings

In addition to its formal meetings in London, its visits to South Africa and the Front-Line States, members of the Group both jointly and individually undertook a series of consultations in Southern Africa, Nigeria and Tanzania, the United States and Europe. As individuals they also had occasional meetings in the course of their work with Commonwealth Heads of Government and Ministers of the seven countries responsible for their appointment to the Group.

Annex 4

The Freedom Charter of South Africa

The 'Freedom Charter' was unanimously adopted at a 'Congress of the People', held in Kliptown, near Johannesburg, on 25 and 26 June, 1955.

The Congress was convened by the African National Congress (ANC), together with the South African Indian Congress, the South African Coloured Peoples' Organization and the Congress of Democrats (an organization of whites supporting the liberation movement). It was attended by 2,888 delegates from throughout South Africa, and was perhaps the most representative gathering ever held in the country.

The Charter was adopted by the four sponsoring organizations as their policy and became a manifesto of their struggle for freedom.

A year later, 156 leaders of these organizations were arrested and charged with 'treason'. They were acquitted after a trial lasting more than four years, but the ANC and the Congress of Democrats were soon banned, while the other two organizations were effectively prevented from legal operation by the banning of their leaders.

The Freedom Charter

We, the people of South Africa, declare for all our country and the world to know:

- that South Africa belongs to all who live in it, black and white, and that no government can justly claim authority unless it is based on the will of all the people;
- that our people have been robbed of their birthright to land, liberty and peace by a form of government founded on injustice and inequality;
- that our country will never be prosperous or free until all our people live in brotherhood, enjoying equal rights and opportunities;
- that only a democratic state, based on the will of all the people, can secure to all their birthright without distinction of colour, race, sex or belief;

And therefore, we the people of South Africa, black and white together – equals, countrymen and brothers – adopt this Freedom Charter. And we pledge ourselves to strive together, sparing neither strength nor courage, until the democratic changes set out here have been won.

The people shall govern!

Every man and woman shall have the right to vote for and to stand as a candidate for all bodies which make laws;

All people shall be entitled to take part in the administration of the country;

The rights of the people shall be the same, regardless of race, colour or sex;

All bodies of minority rule, advisory boards, councils and authorities shall be replaced by democratic organs of self-government.

All national groups shall have equal rights!

There shall be equal status in the bodies of state, in the courts and in the schools for all national groups and races;

All people shall have equal right to use their own languages, and to develop their own folk culture and customs;

All national groups shall be protected by law against insults to their race and national pride;

The preaching and practice of national, race or colour discrimination and contempt shall be a punishable crime;

All apartheid laws and practices shall be set aside.

The people shall share in the country's wealth!

The national wealth of our country, the heritage of all South Africans, shall be restored to the people;

The mineral wealth beneath the soil, the banks and monopoly industry shall be transferred to the ownership of the people as a whole;

All other industry and trade shall be controlled to assist the well-being of the people;

All people shall have equal rights to trade where they choose, to manufacture and to enter all trades, crafts and professions.

The land shall be shared among those who work it!

Restrictions of land ownership on a racial basis shall be ended, and all the land redivided amongst those who work it, to banish famine and land hunger;

The state shall help the peasants with implements, seed, tractors and dams to save the soil and assist the tillers;

Freedom of movement shall be guaranteed to all who work on the land;

All shall have the right to occupy land wherever they choose;

People shall not be robbed of their cattle, and forced labour and farm prisons shall be abolished.

All shall be equal before the law!

No one shall be imprisoned, deported or restricted without a fair trial;

No one shall be condemned by the order of any government official;

The courts shall be representative of all the people;

Imprisonment shall be only for serious crimes against the people, and shall aim at re-education, not vengeance;

The police force and army shall be open to all on an equal basis and shall be the helpers and protectors of the people;

All laws which discriminate on grounds of race, colour or belief shall be repealed.

All shall enjoy equal human rights!

The law shall guarantee to all their rights to speak, to organize, to meet together, to punish, to preach, to worship and to educate their children;

The privacy of the house from police raids shall be protected by law;

All shall be free to travel without restriction from countryside to town, from province to province and from South Africa abroad;

Pass Laws, permits, and all other laws restricting these freedoms, shall be abolished.

There shall be work and security!

All who work shall be free to form unions, to elect their officers and to make wage agreements with their employers;

The state shall recognize the right and duty of all to work, and to draw full unemployment benefits;

Men and women of all races shall receive equal pay for equal work;

There shall be a forty-hour working week, a national minimum wage, paid annual leave, and sick leave for all workers, and maternity leave on full pay for all working mothers;

Miners, domestic workers, farm workers, and civil servants shall have the same rights as all others who work;

Child labour, compound labour, the tot system and contract labour shall be abolished.

The doors of learning and of culture shall be opened!

The government shall discover, develop and encourage national talent for the enhancement of our cultural life;

All the cultural treasures of mankind shall be open to all, by free exchange of books, ideas and contact with other lands;

The aim of education shall be to teach the youth to love their people and their culture, to honour human brotherhood, liberty and peace;

Education shall be free, compulsory, universal and equal for all children;

Higher education and technical training shall be opened to all by means of state allowances and scholarships awarded on the basis of merit;

Adult illiteracy shall be ended by a mass state education plan;

Teachers shall have the rights of other citizens;

The colour bar in cultural life, in sport and in education shall be abolished.

There shall be houses, security and comfort!

All people shall have the rights to live where they choose, to be decently housed, and to bring up their families in comfort, and security;

Unused housing space shall be made available to the people;

Rent and prices shall be lowered, food plentiful and no one shall go hungry;

A preventive health scheme shall be run by the state;

Free medical care and hospitalization shall be provided for all, with special care for mothers and young children;

Slums shall be demolished, and new suburbs built where all have transport, roads, lighting, playing fields, crèches and social centres;

The aged, the orphans, the disabled and the sick shall be cared for by the state;

Rest, leisure and recreation shall be the right of all;

Fenced locations and ghettos shall be abolished, and laws which break up families shall be repealed;

South Africa shall be a fully independent state, which respects the rights and sovereignty of nations;

There shall be peace and friendship!

South Africa shall strive to maintain world peace and the settlement of all international disputes by negotiation – not war;

Peace and friendship amongst all our people shall be secured by upholding the equal rights, opportunities and status of all;

The people of the protectorates – Basutoland, Bechuanaland and Swaziland – shall be free to decide for themselves their own future;

The rights of all the people of Africa to independence and self-government shall be recognized, and shall be the basis of close cooperation;

Let all who love their people and the country now say, as we say here:

'These freedoms we will fight for, side by side, throughout our lives, until we have won our liberty'.

Annex 5

Banning Order on Mrs Winnie Mandela

TO: NOMZAMO WINNIE MANDELA
    802 BLACK VILLAGE
    BRANDFORT

NOTICE IN TERMS OF SECTION 21 OF THE INTERNAL SECURITY ACT, 1982 (ACT 74 OF 1982)

Under and by virtue of the powers vested in me by section 21 of the Internal Security Act, 1982 (Act 74 of 1982), I hereby order you for the period from 2 July 1983 to 30 June 1988, both dates inclusive, to report to the officer in charge of the Brandfort Police Station, on every Monday between 06h00 and 18h00: Provided that if such Monday falls on a public holiday, you shall report on the following day not being a public holiday.

Given under my hand at Cape Town this 18th day of June 1983.

L. LE GRANGE
MINISTER OF LAW AND ORDER

Note: The Magistrate, Brandfort, has in terms of section 21 of Act 74 of 1982 been empowered to authorize exceptions to the prohibitions contained in this notice.

TO: NOMZAMO WINNIE MANDELA
    802 BLACK VILLAGE
    BRANDFORT

NOTICE IN TERMS OF SECTION 19(1)(a) OF THE INTERNAL SECURITY ACT, 1982 (ACT 74 OF 1982)

Under and by virtue of the powers vested in me by section 19(1)(a) of the Internal Security Act, 1982 (Act 74 of 1982), I hereby prohibit you for the period from 2 July 1983 to 30 June 1988, both dates inclusive, from –

(1) absenting yourself from –
  (a) the residential premises situate at lot No. 802 in the Brandfort Black village described in Government Notice No. 212 dated 16 February 1962, at any time, except –

      (i) between 06h00 and 19h30 on any day not being a Saturday, Sunday or public holiday;

     (ii) between 06h00 and 15h30 on any Saturday not being a public holiday;

(b) the municipal area of Brandfort;

(2) being within –

(a) any Black area, that is to say –

      (i) any Scheduled Black Area as defined in the Black Land Act, 1913 (Act 27 of 1913);

     (ii) any land of which the South African Development Trust, referred to in section 4 of the Development Trust and Land Act, 1936 (Act 18 of 1936), is the registered owner or any land held in trust for a Black Tribal Community in terms of the said Development Trust and Land Act, 1936;

    (iii) any location, Black hostel or Black village defined and set apart under the Blacks (Urban Areas) Consolidation Act, 1945 (Act 25 of 1945);

    (iv) any area approved for the residence of Blacks in terms of section 9(2)(h) of the Blacks (Urban Areas) Consolidation Act, 1945 (Act 25 of 1945);

     (v) any township defined and set apart for the occupation of Blacks in terms of the Regulations for the Administration and Control of Townships in Black Areas, promulgated in Proclamation R293 of 16 November 1962,

except the Brandfort Black village described in Government Notice No. 212 dated 16 February 1962;

(b) any compound for Blacks;

(c) any area set apart under any law for the occupation of Coloured or Asiatic persons;

(d) the premises of any factory as defined in the Factories, Machinery and Building Work Act, 1941 (Act 22 of 1941);

(e) any place which constitutes the premises on which any publication as defined in the Internal Security Act, 1982, is prepared, compiled, printed or published;

(f) any place which constitutes the premises of any organization referred to in Part I or I I of the Annexure to Government Notice R2130 of 28 December 1962, as amended by Government Notice R1947 of 27 November 1964, and any place which constitutes premises on which the premises of any such organization are situate;

(g) any place or area which constitutes the premises on which any public or private university, university college, college, school or other educational institution is situate;

(h) any place or area which constitutes the premises of any division of the Supreme Court of South Africa established under the Supreme Court Act, 1959 (Act 59 of 1959), or any court established under the provisions of the Magistrates' Courts Act, 1944 (Act 32 of 1944), except for the purpose of –

    (i) applying to a magistrate for an exception to any prohibition in force against you under the Internal Security Act, 1982;

    (ii) attending any criminal proceedings in which you are required to appear as an accused or a witness;

    (iii) attending any civil proceedings in which you are a plaintiff, petitioner, applicant, defendant, respondent or other party or in which you are required to appear as a witness;

(3) performing any of the following acts –

  (a) preparing, compiling, printing, publishing, disseminating or transmitting in any manner whatsoever any publication as defined in the Internal Security Act, 1982;

  (b) participating or assisting in any manner whatsoever in the preparation, compilation, printing, publication, dissemination or transmission of any publication as so defined;

  (c) contributing, preparing, compiling or transmitting in any manner whatsoever any matter for publication in any publication as so defined;

  (d) assisting in any manner whatsoever in the preparation, compilation or transmission of any matter for publication in any publication as so defined;

  (e) (i) preparing, compiling, printing, publishing, disseminating or transmitting in any manner whatsoever any document (which shall include any book, pamphlet, record, list, placard, poster, drawing, photograph or picture which is not a publication within the meaning of paragraph (3)(a) above); or

    (ii) participating or assisting in any manner whatsoever in the preparation, compilation, printing, publication, dissemination or transmission of any such document,

    in which, *inter alia* –

      (aa) any form of State or any principle or policy of the Government of a State is propagated, defended, attacked, criticized, discussed or referred to;

> > (bb) any matter is contained concerning any unlawful organization as defined in section 1 of the Internal Security Act, 1982, or any organization referred to in Part I or II of the Annexure to Government Notice R2130 of 28 December 1962, as amended by Government Notice R1947 of 27 November 1964; or
> > (cc) any matter is contained which is likely to engender feelings of hostility between different population groups or parts of population groups of the Republic of South Africa;
>
> (f) giving any educational instruction in any manner or form to any person other than a person of whom you are a parent;
> (g) taking part in any manner whatsoever in the activities or affairs of any organization referred to in Part I or II of the Annexure to Government Notice R2130 of 28 December 1962, as amended by Government Notice R1947 of 27 November 1964;

(4) communicating in any manner whatsoever with any person whose name appears on any list compiled in terms of section 4(10) of the Internal Security Act, 1950 (Act 44 of 1950), or the consolidated list referred to in section 16 of the Internal Security Act, 1982, or in respect of whom any prohibition under the Internal Security Act, 1982 is in force.

Given under my hand at Cape Town this 18th day of June 1983.

L. LE GRANGE
MINISTER OF LAW AND ORDER

Note: (1) The Magistrate, Brandfort, has in terms of section 19(1) of Act 74 of 1982 been empowered to authorize exceptions to the prohibitions contained in this notice.

(2) In terms of section 25(2) of the said Act you may, at any time within a period of fourteen days as from the date on which this notice is delivered or tendered to you, make written representations to the Minister of Law and Order relating to the prohibitions contained in this notice and you may also, within the said period submit in writing any other information relating to the circumstances of your case. You may also, in terms of section 38(4) of the Act, apply in writing to the Board of Review to present oral evidence before the Board of Review. The address of the Board of Review is: The Secretary of the Board of Review, Private Bag X655, PRETORIA, 0001.

STATEMENT IN TERMS OF SECTION 25(1) OF THE
INTERNAL SECURITY ACT, 1982 (ACT 74 OF 1982)

(a) Reasons for the notice issued in terms of section 19(1)(a) of the
Internal Security Act, 1982, to NOMZAMO WINNIE
MANDELA:

I am satisfied that the said NOMZAMO WINNIE MAN-
DELA is likely to propagate or promote activities which endanger
or are calculated to endanger the security of the State or the maintenance of law and order.

(b) Information which induced me to issue the said notice:

The information which induced me to issue the said notice cannot,
in my opinion, be disclosed without detriment to the public interest.

Given under my hand at Cape Town this 18th day of June 1983.

L. LE GRANGE
MINISTER OF LAW AND ORDER

———————

TO: NOMZAMO WINNIE MANDELA
    802 BLACK VILLAGE
    BRANDFORT

NOTICE IN TERMS OF SECTION 20(a) OF THE
INTERNAL SECURITY ACT, 1982 (ACT 74 OF 1982)

Under and by virtue of the powers vested in me by section 20(a) of the
Internal Security Act, 1982 (Act 74 of 1982), I hereby prohibit you for
the period from 2 July 1983 to 30 June 1988, both dates inclusive,
from attending within the Republic of South Africa –

(1) any gathering as contemplated in subparagraph (i) of the said
    section 20; or
(2) any gathering as contemplated in subparagraph (ii) of the said
    section 20, of the nature, class or kind set out below:
  (a) Any social gathering, that is to say, any gathering at which the
      persons present also have social intercourse with one another;
  (b) any political gathering, that is to say, any gathering at which any
      form of State or any principle or policy of the Government of a
      State is propagated, defended, attacked, criticized or discussed;

(c) any gathering of pupils or students assembled for the purpose of being instructed, trained or addressed by you.

Given under my hand at Cape Town this 18th day of June 1983.

L. LE GRANGE
MINISTER OF LAW AND ORDER

Note: (1) The Magistrate, Brandfort, has in terms of section 20 of Act 74 of 1982 been empowered to authorize exceptions to the prohibitions contained in this notice.

(2) In terms of section 25(2) of the said Act you may, at any time within a period of fourteen days as from the date on which this notice is delivered or tendered to you, make written representations to the Minister of Law and Order relating to the prohibitions contained in this notice and you may also, within the said period, submit in writing any other information relating to the circumstances of your case. You may also, in terms of section 38(4) of the Act, apply in writing to the Board of Review to present oral evidence before the Board of Review. The address of the Board of Review is: The Secretary of the Board of Review, Private Bag X655, Pretoria, 0001.

STATEMENT IN TERMS OF SECTION 25(1) OF THE INTERNAL SECURITY ACT, 1982 (ACT 74 OF 1982)

(a) Reasons for the notice issued in terms of section 20(a) of the Internal Security Act, 1982, to NOMZAMO WINNIE MANDELA:

I am satisfied that the said NOMZAMO WINNIE MANDELA is likely to propagate or promote activities which endanger or are calculated to endanger the security of the State or the maintenance of law and order.

(b) Information which induced me to issue the said notice:

The information which induced me to issue the said notice cannot, in my opinion, be disclosed without detriment to the public interest.

Given under my hand at Cape Town this 18th day of June 1983.

L. LE GRANGE
MINISTER OF LAW AND ORDER

Annexure B

TO: KOMZAMO WINNIE MANDELA
    BRANDFORT

NOTICE IN TERMS OF SECTION 24 OF THE INTERNAL SECURITY ACT, 1982 (ACT 74 OF 1982)

I hereby, in terms of section 24 of the Internal Security Act, 1982 –

(1) amend the notice issued in terms of section 19(1)(a) of the said Act on 18 June 1983 and delivered to you on 29 June 1983, by –

    (a) the substitution for paragraph (1) of the following paragraph:
        '(1) being within any of the following magisterial districts, namely Johannesburg and Roodepoort';

    (b) the deletion of subparagraphs (a), (b), (c), (d) and (h) of paragraph (2);

(2) amend the notice issued in terms of section 20(a) of the said Act on 16 June 1983 and delivered to you on 29 June 1983, by the deletion of paragraph (1) and subparagraph (a) of paragraph (2);

(3) withdraw the notice issued in terms of section 21 of the said Act on 18 June 1983 and delivered to you on 29 June 1983.

Signed at Cape Town this 20th day of December 1985.

L. LE GRANGE
MINISTER OF LAW AND ORDER

Annex 6

Announcements by the State President on Constitutional Development

Constitutional Goal

'The Government's general constitutional goal is, while maintaining security, stability and self-determination for each group, to give all the country's people a say in decision-making that affects their interests. This applies to all the population communities of South Africa.' (25 January 1985)

Undivided South Africa

'I thus finally confirm that my Party and I are committed to the principle of a united South Africa, one citizenship and a universal franchise within structures chosen by South Africans . . .' (30 September 1985)

'The over-riding common denominator is our mutual interest in each other's freedom and well-being. Our peace and prosperity is indivisible.' (15 August 1985)

'We accept an undivided Republic of South Africa where all regions and communities within its boundaries form part of the South African state, with the right to participate in institutions to be negotiated collectively.' (31 January 1985)

Democracy

'In the constitutional field I want to stress that the Government is resolved to pursue peaceful and democratic solutions that satisfy the requirements of fairness and justice.' (25 January 1985)

'We believe in democratic institutions of government.' (15 August 1985)

'Solutions must be democratic, but in this regard I wish to join the ranks of other leaders who agree that solutions are not to be found in cliched models although they could include elements of known models.' (30 September 1985)

'We believe that a democratic system of government, which must accommodate all legitimate political aspirations of all the South African communities, must be negotiated.' (31 January 1986)

Apartheid

'If apartheid means
– political domination of one group over another;
– the exclusion of any community from the political decision-making process;
– injustice and inequality in the opportunities available to any community;
– racial discrimination and encroachment upon human dignity;
then the South African Government shares in the rejection of the concept.' (30 September 1985)

'We have outgrown the outdated colonial system of paternalism as well as the outdated concept of apartheid.' (31 January 1986)

Power-Sharing

'My Government stated clearly that all groups and communities within the geographical area of this state must obtain representation to the highest level without domination of the one over the other. Therefore I do not understand why the Government is time and again still expected to say that it is prepared to share its decision-making power with other communities. It is accepted National Party Policy . . .' (30 September 1985)

'The peoples of the Republic of South Africa form one nation. But our nation is a nation of minorities. Given the multi-cultural nature of South African society, this of necessity implies participation by all communities; the sharing of power between these communities; but also the devolution of power as far as possible; and the protection of minority rights, without one group dominating another.' (31 January 1986)

Participation in Government

'Now let me say explicitly that I believe in participation of all the South African communities on matters of common concern. I believe there should exist structures to reach this goal of co-responsibility and participation.' (15 August 1985)

'It is evident that units will have to be recognized on a geographical and group basis. This obviously also includes the black urban communities who, for constitutional purposes, are recognized as political entities. Each such unit should have autonomy on matters that only affect that unit, while the units on central level should jointly manage matters of mutual concern.' (30 September 1985)

'All South Africans must be placed in a position where they can participate in government through their elected representatives.' (31 January 1986)

No Domination

'We are committed to co-operative co-existence . . . But this is possible only within a system in which there is no domination of one population group over another, which in turn requires self-determination for each group over its own affairs and joint responsibility for and co-operation on common interests.' (25 January 1985)

'But I know for a fact that most leaders in their own right in South Africa and reasonable South Africans will not accept the principle of one-man-one-vote in a unitary system. That would lead to domination of one over the others and it would lead to chaos.' (15 August 1985)

Protection of Minorities

'We believe in the protection of minorities.' (15 August 1985)

'Any constitutional dispensation will have to take into consideration the multi-cultural nature of the composition of our population in this country, and that any dispensation will have to ensure that one group is not placed in a position where it can dominate other groups. The protection of minority groups will thus have to be ensured.' (30 September 1985)

'We are involved in the mutual pursuance of both equal rights for individuals and security for each group. The ways in which the fundamental rights of individuals and groups ... can be protected, are therefore an essential element of the Government's agenda for constitutional reform.' (30 September 1985)

'We believe in the sovereignty of the law as the basis for the protection of the fundamental rights of individuals as well as groups. We believe in the sanctity and indivisibility of law and the just application thereof.' (31 January 1986)

'There can be no peace, freedom and democracy without law. Any future system must conform with the requirements of a civilized legal order, and must ensure access to the courts and equality before the law.' (31 January 1986)

'We believe that human dignity, life, liberty and property of all must be protected, regardless of colour, race, creed or religion.' (31 January 1986)

National States

'Co-operation with the independent states within the multilateral dispensation will, in line with the current trend, be further extended as a level at which the governments concerned are given a say regarding actions by the RSA that affect them, and vice versa.' (25 January 1985)

'The Government respects the decision of the four states that previously formed part of the Republic, to take independence. As a result of the large degree of interdependence between the independent states and the Republic, the Government nevertheless acknowledges the possibility of co-operation with these states in an overall framework.' (30 September 1985)

'Independence will remain the goal in the case of the self-governing states, but since the Government does not intend forcing this on anyone, there will be increasing co-operation with self-governing national states within collective structures.' (25 January 1985)

'Should any of the black National States therefore prefer not to accept independence, such states or communities will remain a part of the South African nation, are South African citizens and should be accommodated within political institutions within the boundaries of the Republic of South Africa.' (15 August 1985)

'The Republic of South Africa forms one state. It is an explicit implication of the Government's view that independence will not be forced on the self-governing regions and that they form part of the Republic until they should decide to become independent.' (30 September 1985)

Urban Blacks

'It has been decided to treat such (black) communities for constitutional purposes as entities which in their own right ... must be given political participations and a say at higher levels.' (25 January 1985)

'I admit that the acceptance by my Government of the permanence of black communities in urban areas outside the National States means that a solution will have to be found for their legitimate rights.' (15 August 1985)

Citizenship

'We must consequently accept the South African citizenship of those black persons who lost their citizenship because of the independence of Transkei, Bophuthatswana, Venda and Ciskei, but who permanently reside in South Africa.' (11 September 1985)

'The South African Government is prepared to negotiate with these four Governments about restoring the South African citizenship of members of the black communities residing within the borders of Transkei, Bophuthatswana, Venda and Ciskei, who lost their citizenship as a result of independence. We propose that this be done on the basis of dual citizenship ...' (30 September 1985)

'We accept one citizenship for all South Africans, implying equal treatment and opportunities.' (31 January 1986)

Overall Framework

'To avoid unnecessary fragmentation at the constitutional level the Government has decided that, in the longer term, efforts should be made to co-operate on matters of common interest within the same overall framework with the various political entities that find themselves within the South African context.' (25 January 1985)

Negotiation

'It is necessary that the existing mechanisms for negotiation be improved and that the process of negotiation be substantially extended. I have therefore decided to establish an informal, non-statutory forum ... to create a favourable basis for negotiations aimed at arriving at mutually acceptable development steps in the constitutional field.' (25 January 1985)

'It is my considered opinion that any future constitutional dispensation providing for participation by all South African citizens should be negotiated.' (15 August 1985)

'I say it would be wrong to be prescriptive as to structures within which participation will have to take place in future.' (15 August 1985)

'It is the conviction of the Government that the structures in which this co-operation will take place, must be the result of negotiation with the leaders of all the communities.' (30 September 1985)

'If the need exists among the leaders of black communities to participate within the President's Council ... I am willing to reconsider the structuring and the functions of the President's Council to make provision for their participation.' (30 September 1985)

National Statutory Council

'I now wish to announce that I intend to negotiate the establishment of a national statutory council which will meet under my chairmanship.

I propose that this council should consist of representatives of the South African Government, representatives of the Governments of the self-governing National States, as well as leaders of other black communities and interest groups.

Pending the creation of constitutional structures jointly to be agreed upon for our multi-cultural society, this council should consider and advise on matters of common concern, including proposed legislation of such matters.

This council can meet under the chairmanship of the State President as often as needed.' (31 January 1986)

Annex 7

An Extract from Address by State President P. W. Botha, DMS, before the President's Council Cape Town, 15 May 1986

Norms and Values

Consequently, in the interest of South Africa and our various population groups, I want to spell out emphatically certain important principles which are not negotiable.

Firstly, whatever negotiated solutions we can produce will have to be implemented by Parliament since negotiated reform must be implemented constitutionally. This includes the possibility of general elections or a referendum, in the case of drastic deviation from already accepted policies.

Secondly, the Government subscribes to certain fundamental norms and values by which it will be guided throughout the process of negotiation in the belief that a negotiated settlement is only possible within the parameters of these norms and values.

It will also be guided by these norms and values while it continues to govern the country as a civilized state.

These norms and values include the following which will have to be entrenched in any new dispensation:

1. The realization of the democratic ideal since it is the Government's accepted principle that only democratic institutions can meet the demands of justice and fairness.

   This means that a democratic dispensation of government which must accommodate the legitimate political aspirations of all South Africa's communities must be designed and implemented.

   Such a dispensation must take cognizance of and reflect the multi-cultural nature of the South African society and must provide for visible and effective protection of minority groups and the rights against domination and for self-determination for such groups and communities.

   South Africa is a country of minorities and a multi-cultural society. Its diversity is a fact that must be accepted.

   The Goverment is committed to devise such democratic solutions in co-operation with South Africans who are also committed to peaceful and democratic solutions and who reject violence as a means of achieving political goals.

In this respect it is the Government's conviction that only purposeful broadening of democracy of the South African society at large and accompanying socio-economic reform can ensure lasting peace and stability.

2. Adherence to Christian values and civilized norms with recognition and protection of freedom of faith and worship. This principle is a cornerstone of our existence as a civilized state.

3. Maintenance of the sovereignty and the integrity of the Republic of South Africa. This requires well disciplined and suitably equipped Security Forces. It means that South Africa must be able to protect the integrity of its borders, as well as to defend its people against internationally organized terrorism and to maintain law and order. Nobody must underestimate our determination in this regard. As a regional power in Southern Africa, this is our indisputable duty.

4. The sanctity and indivisibility of law and the just application thereof, the independence of the judiciary and the equality of all under the law.

5. Liberty as a cornerstone of true democracy which must manifest itself on different levels.

Firstly, on the personal and individual level which also implies respect for and the protection of the human dignity, life and property of all.

Secondly, liberty on the group and community level which implies respect for and the promotion and protection of the right to self-determination of population groups and peoples.

Thirdly, liberty on the state and national level to safeguard the integrity and freedom of the country and to secure the protection of our citizens through the application of civilized standards of justice, order and security.

True democracy for the Republic of South Africa and all its peoples, individually and collectively, must recognize each of these components of freedom since the absence of such recognition will diminish, not increase, the freedom of our peoples.

6. Furtherance of private enterprise and effective competition as well as confidence in our economy.

7. Elimination of discrimination implying selection for unfavourable treatment or prejudicial action on the basis of race, cultural affiliation or religious conviction.